WHAT COLLEGE DIDN'T TEACH ME

By: Amanda Maggiore

Jordan,
 Embrace the small opportunities! Enjoy life!
♥ Amanda Maggiore

What College Didn't Teach Me

Copyright © 2022 by Amanda Maggiore.

All rights reserved. No part of this publication may be reproduced, distributed, or transmitted in any form or by any means, including photocopying, recording, or other electronic or mechanical methods, without the prior written permission of the publisher, except in the case of brief quotations embodied in critical reviews and certain other noncommercial uses permitted by copyright law. For permission requests, write to the publisher, addressed "Attention: Permissions Coordinator," on the website below.

ISBN: 979-8-9871739-0-9 (Paperback)
ISBN: 979-8-9871739-1-6 (Ebook)

Library of Congress Cataloging-in-Publication Data has been applied for.

Front cover image designed by Freepik - Freepik.com.
Book design by Gina Neilsen.
Edited by Valerie Valentine.

Every attempt has been made to properly source all quotes.

First printing edition 2022.

Publisher - Maggiore Marketing Inc.

www.whatcollegedidntteachme.com

ACKNOWLEDGEMENTS

To Mom, Dad, and Kristen, thank you for your continuous support and unconditional love for me. You have always pushed me to pursue what I want and stood by my side each step of the way. Without your loud cheers, encouraging words, and gigantic hugs, I wouldn't be where I am today. You helped shape who I am today. I love you.

To my closest family and friends, you have watched me grow and learn through the years. The ups, the downs, and all that falls in between. Thank you for being by my side through every event in life. You keep me going day in and day out. You all are a tremendous blessing in my life, and I am eternally grateful.

All my love,
Amanda Gracie

Table of Contents

Introduction	01
Chapter 1: Initial Shock	03
Chapter 2: Adaptability	08
Chapter 3: Health	16
Chapter 4: Dating	32
Chapter 5: Friendships	61
Chapter 6: Support System	72
Chapter 7: Communication	77
Chapter 8: Career	84
Chapter 9: Financials	101
Chapter 10: Goals and Dreams	122
Chapter 11: Immerse into the Culture	131
Chapter 12: Travel	137
Chapter 13: Accountability	144
Chapter 14: Mindset	151
Chapter 15: Live Your Best Life	169
Author Biography	171

Introduction

This may surprise many, but college is not the place to get more knowledge (remember, "girls go to college to get more knowledge and boys go to Jupiter to get more stupider" in our younger years?). Mass producers create the education system with their expensive textbooks and generic ideas. These publishers are businesses determined to make money by telling students what they "need" to know for their future. They have already lived out their working years and still believe what they learned twenty years ago is relevant to our era. These manufacturers control what you know, as they strategically create the content you read and interact with daily. Universities buy into this theory and force instructors to use these cumbersome books with students.

How many classes have you had up to this point in your life that you know were useless? A lot, I am sure. The textbooks cost an arm and a leg for four months of use, yet sometimes you don't even open them. I remember taking classes, I was not even remotely interested in because superiors told me to do so. Courses that were supposed to "increase my knowledge" in a topic I did not give a crap about. I remember thinking, "Why am I wasting my time on something so impractical to me?"

I am here to tell you that most life lessons and skills are not learned by sitting in a classroom or, better yet, at Zoom University. Instead, they are discovered and nurtured by worldly experiences and relevant research on topics YOU are interested in.

Your whole life, you have been told what to learn and study. The system has developed you into a robot by giving you the structure they think you need. But, as we have grown, the capabilities of learning just about anything sit at the edge of our fingertips—the gift of the internet.

Learning new things is great, but experiencing them makes an even more significant impact on your life. When you work to fulfill a purposeful life, you will begin to notice the development in yourself. The greatest gift you give to yourself in life is YOU. You determine your outcome and future. You hold the power to make all the decisions to get you to where you want to be. Regardless of your circumstances, change in your life is possible. You have more influence over yourself and your path than you even know. With the incredible power you currently hold, you can create a life you will be proud of one day.

You are entering the newest stage of life with French doors wide open, waiting for your arrival. I will give you the extra nudge you need to make those life-changing plans. Are you ready for your journey ahead?

CHAPTER 1: INITIAL SHOCK

Congratulations. You did it. You made it to the end of college. How did the time fly by so fast? The memories absorbed, the stress endured, and the once-in-a-lifetime experiences have led to this final moment. I want to start by saying how proud I am of you. You have accomplished what seemed impossible and have proven to yourself that you can finish strong. It is not always easy, but I hope you understand that these times will shape who you are long after walking across the stage.

It is hard to think back to your first day, a scared freshman wandering the campus, trying not to look like a total freak while searching for the right classroom. Anxiety, nervousness, and excitement kept you powering through those trying first few weeks. You quickly learned your new life's ins and outs that shaped the rest of your time—because you had to. You grew through these years and have developed into something your younger self could never comprehend. Here you stand today, thinking back to all your beautiful memories created. Don't let them go. Cherish them and celebrate them. These moments will cling to your heart as you go through life.

So at this moment, you are asking yourself the million-dollar question: "What now?"

Well, I can tell you that no matter if you went to a prestigious Ivy League school or a local community college, you are not prepared for what you are about to experience. You might say,

"Change is painful, but nothing is as painful as staying stuck somewhere you don't belong." -Mandy Hale

"But my education was amazing!" I am sure it was. So was mine. But this is bigger than your soon-to-be alma mater. This is a crazy thing called life that is waiting for you.

There are many adjustments you will have to make. Ones you might recognize and others you will notice as they are happening. For example, the weird feeling of not having your roommate sleep five feet from you every night hits hard when you are in a room alone. The lack of laughter and extra noise makes the silence louder. Coordinating who is doing what for dinner suddenly turns into you debating whether to cook or get takeout for the third time this week. You have left the life that absorbed your entire being in a matter of days. With a flip of a switch, you are now in an unfamiliar space with no safety net. It is all on you.

Breaking Away from College

It can be tough to separate yourself from the college lifestyle, especially if you are living close by. Being stuck in college life can prevent you from growing into your future self. You don't want to be the person trying to stretch out their college days as long as possible. We all have seen that one person that lingers at every frat party, Thirsty Thursday, and Homecoming event after they should have been long gone. They attempt to relive the chapter of life that should have closed long ago. Keeping yourself in the same atmosphere will hinder your growth and potential to make something meaningful of yourself.

"Moving on is easy. It's staying moved on that's trickier."
-Katerina Stoykova Klemer

The college chapter is hard to leave, but turning the page is thrilling once you take the plunge. Removing yourself from the college scene will allow you to cherish your memories and recognize that it is time to move on to bigger and better things.

Think about all the generations that have gone through college already. It would be weird to see a fifty-year-old still attending events like they are a student, right? You know there would be many judgmental whispers about this person. You don't need to leave the people and memories entirely in the past to forget; instead, keep them close to your heart and let them fuel your passion for starting the next phase of life.

Accepting this new challenge of entering the adult world is more complicated than you might think. We want the fun and comfortable environment to follow us, but all good things must end. Force yourself to keep what is essential in your mind and heart while taking the first step into your new reality. By removing yourself from your previous chapter, you are already setting the stage for what is to come.

You might believe you just had the best years of your life while in school. Up until this point, they probably are. But just wait, you have not seen anything yet. If you think time passed by in a few blinks while attending college, there is no slowing down when you get out. You are about to experience what real life has in store. You are no longer living in a bubble.

"Fear tricks us into living a boring life." -Donald Miller

The world is at your feet, offering everything you could want.

Unfortunately, opportunities won't always find you, and sometimes you must go seeking what you desire.

Make yourself into the person you have always wanted to be in this new life. You have the freedom and expertise to live out your dreams. This stage should not be taken for granted, as these are some of the most influential years yet. This is the time to focus on yourself and make life worth living.

Your journey is now beginning, whether you're ready or not. Life is constantly moving, and it won't wait for you. So get up, and embrace what is ahead for your personal story.

"Letting go is hard but being free is beautiful." -Wilder Poetry

CHAPTER 2: ADAPTABILITY

You sat through many classes; some you liked, some you didn't. You adapted to many different teaching styles throughout your time in school. However, this adaptability is only minor compared to what's needed for your life ahead. When you are facing some substantial life changes, that is when you learn to adapt quickly to your new surroundings and environment. When vital elements in your life change, it is either fight-or-flight mode. You have probably already experienced it with significant life events such as losing a loved one or going through challenging situations with family and friends. I hate to be the bearer of bad news, but change is inevitable now more than ever in the big-kid world. You will go through battles you never even imagined, and you must learn how to quickly adjust your actions and thoughts to process the situation thoroughly.

Even when you think you have it all figured out and life is going the way you have always wanted, a wrench, or three, gets thrown into the mix, altering your plans altogether. And you know what?

That is okay.

Learning to embrace change is a skill that did not always come easy to me. Nevertheless, I purposely forced myself into uncomfortable situations because that change is what I needed to grow. I knew that if I felt comfortable with my situation, I would never be able to break free of my current comfort bubble that was limiting my potential.

"There are far better things ahead than any we leave behind." -C.S. Lewis

The extreme of adaptability can vary with every situation. For example, I chose to move from Denver, Colorado, to Dallas, Texas, where I hadn't spent more than a week. I caught myself trying to comprehend the logic of moving, and I knew then that I had to do it, or I would never change. Or on a less severe note, I had to think on my feet when I learned some alarming information about the company I was working for right out of college. I knew I had to leave to save my career, but leaving a stable job sounded like the craziest idea. I listened to my gut, so I ripped the band-aid off and ran like the wind. I mentally prepared myself to be job hunting for a while, so I had to be more frugal with my money just in case I did not find a job immediately. I was lucky to land a role I love a week after quitting.

Your adaptation skills have only progressed as you have aged because you have experienced more. You learned to let go of the reins and trust that your intuition would get you through the trying times. Sometimes, without even noticing it, you willingly put yourself in a vulnerable situation to make yourself a more well-rounded person.

The person you were four years ago is not the same person reading this book. Hell, you aren't even the same person you were yesterday. Your life is moving at a million miles a minute right in front of your eyes. That is the exciting part.

Your growth can be subconscious until you wake up and see the

"Adaptability is not imitation. It means power of resistance and assimilation."
-Mahatma Gandhi

changes you have made in life staring back at you in the mirror. The positive difference you see in yourself is how you know you are pursuing the right path in life.

This book will explain the importance of adaptability and breaking out of the comfort zone. To start your life on a good note, you must quickly force yourself to conform to the situations around you. Not everything will go right all the time. You understand by now what facing severe lows, and highs in life feels like. The constant rollercoaster will not stop, but you can change how you react and handle situations, good or bad. Wrenches will get thrown into your plans, always. Whatever roadblock comes your way will only strengthen you and prepare you more for the future. You will learn valuable lessons without even realizing it.

Be prepared to do things you have never done before to conform to your surroundings. Let's say you moved to a new city on your own. You must acclimate to make this transition easier. Even if you are moving back home to save money, you will have to adjust and prepare to live with your parents again. Going from four years of freedom with no one to report to, then having your parents ask you a question every time you step toward the front door can be mentally exhausting. Set boundaries with your parents immediately and have clear and open communication about what they expect and allow while you live at home. You can adjust how you go about your day-to-day if you

"Adaptability is the simple secret of survival." -Jessica Hagedorn

understand the expectations. Adapting to your surroundings will make you more versatile and allow you to better handle changing aspects of life.

"When we allow ourselves to adapt to different situations, life is easier."
-Catherine Pulsifer

How Am I Going To Adapt?

With all the new experiences you have coming up in life, I want you to think about the steps you will take to prepare for unique situations. What areas of your life will change when you start your new journey? How will you adapt?

_____
_____
_____
_____
_____
_____
_____
_____
_____
_____
_____
_____
_____
_____
_____
_____
_____
_____
_____
_____
_____
_____
_____
_____
_____
_____
_____

You will encounter many situations and feelings that you may never have been through before. Your twenties are about the question, "What am I even doing?" We are in the same boat, not knowing what to do with each day. We have lived through a structured life where elders and authorities have told us what to do and where we need to be. Once you have entered this stage of life, no one is telling you what to do, forcing you to figure it out. That, itself, is a gift. You get to choose how you spend your precious time. You get to determine your daily outcome.

Give yourself grace. I learned a difficult lesson when I first was on my own post-college. I thought everything I was doing had to be completely perfect because this was the adult world, and I could not mess up anymore. For instance, I worked tiring hours to create excellent work for my job, only to be instructed to redo it. I thought I had to push myself past the point of exhaustion in the gym every time I walked in the door to have that perfect young-twenties body. I put a lot of pressure on myself to make friends, which resulted in the feeling of being desperate.

Understand that all of the pieces in your life take time to develop. If you are starting your first big-kid job, know that you are not going to be the best at it, and it is going to take hard work and dedication to get to the level that is satisfying to you. Be gentle with your words to yourself, as they will set the tone for how you perform in life. If you are too cruel and put an insane amount of pressure on yourself, your burnout rate will be high, your errors

"Intelligence is the ability to adapt to change." -Stephen Hawking

will increase, and you won't have that feeling of fulfillment. Work hard each day, but don't push yourself past your limits. Set boundaries for yourself, as these will help you find an appropriate work-life balance for your path.

Going through the motions of your twenties can be draining on the mind and body. There is abundant change happening all around you at a rapid speed. Your life is evolving, and it can be hard to keep up mentally and physically. So your number-one priority should always be taking care of yourself.

"If we don't change, we don't grow. If we don't grow, we aren't really living."
-Anatole Franc

CHAPTER 3: HEALTH

Mental Health

We have all been there. We are fighting to keep going at the current pace of life but know it is not sustainable. One rough occurrence after another keeps happening. The long, exhausting bad days continue with no end in sight. The black holes seem to swallow us and make it almost impossible to climb out. Every battle you have endured has led you to this point. You have already been through a lot that has affected your mental health. And the unfortunate part is that it follows you to your next chapter.

I firmly believe college does not help your mental health. Why? A few reasons. The classes that you take have expectations for you. They are asking for a certain number of hours per week to study to succeed. If you can slide by without having to dedicate an enormous number of hours to studying, you are gifted. Many of us must spend our free hours reviewing the material to get a good grade in the class. Even if you put every free minute you have into studying, and you still fail, the school does not care.

Think about all the time wasted on a subject that most likely will be irrelevant once you leave college. You stressed out, worked yourself up, and had to put school ahead of taking care of yourself. You avoided sleep, filled your body with enough caffeine to last you until age thirty, and missed out on core memories to attempt to pass a class. If you happened to miss

"Not until we are lost do we begin to understand ourselves."
-Henry David Thoreau

class for some legitimate reason, they would make you feel bad about it.

One of my biggest pet peeves was when a professor would say their class should be the main priority over everything: personal life, athletics, health, you name it. Being told that a three-day-a-week class is more important than a family emergency is outrageous and cruel. Schools and professors forget that these beliefs have a lasting impact on students throughout life. This mentality sets up students to believe that work will always be more important than anything going on in life.

The pressure that schools and athletics put on students is unrealistic. They expect you to do well in classes, focus on your sport, which is almost a full-time job, work so you can support yourself, and graduate in a decent amount of time.

Overwork and unrealistic expectations create constant stress and takes a toll on young students, causing burnout. I think back to my days in college, and I do not know how I balanced two jobs, full-time school, and a regular social schedule. Think about how much you had to juggle at once. As a result, your tenacious attitude has grown, but your mental health most likely suffered during that time.

College does not teach you to prioritize yourself. Unfortunately, we must learn this behavior on our own or from peers and family.

"A healthy outside starts from the inside." -Robert Urich

The sooner you take charge of your mental health and realize what you need to be happy in life, the more prepared you will be for the future. Taking the reins of your mental health starts with baby steps. You cannot throw yourself into the fire of good mental practices all at once. Your choices must actively reflect what you are trying to change and improve upon.

The beginning stages should be small actions that begin to shift your mindset and provide clarity for you. One of your first actions should be recognizing what your environment offers. Think about it for a second. How lucky are you that you woke up breathing this morning? Do you understand how many people wish they were in your same boat? You are doing very well if you have a consistent roof over your head, food on the table, and fresh water at your disposal. Consider all the lucky cards you have been dealt and recognize how good you have it, so much better than someone else. So many people would kill to have a week in your shoes.

Start each day by saying, writing, or even singing ten things you are thankful for in your life. Changing your mindset to contain more positive thoughts will change your entire perception, one day at a time.

"Self-care is not selfish. You cannot serve from an empty vessel."
-Eleanor Brown

GRATITUDE

TODAY I'M GRATEFUL FOR ...

The internal and external battles, big or small, that we face every day can be fought with extreme positivity, hard work, and help. Do self check-ins often to analyze how you are doing. Be honest with yourself, and don't try to mask the true feelings that are buried deep inside you. Participating in self-evaluations regularly might sound silly, but it can make a huge difference in your mental state.

Having a positive mindset will carry you through life. Of course, there will always be roadblocks and struggles, but if you look at the glass as half full in every situation, your mindset will slowly start to think more positively.

Breaking the negative thought cycle is total war; that's why consistency is vital. Positivity comes in all forms. Being positive about your work, yourself, your living situation, and so much more makes a difference in how you view your reality. Practice ways to be positive daily and take every problem that comes to you with grace.

Keeping a straight head on your shoulders takes effort. Sometimes, the chemicals don't allow us to be okay when we want to be. You must know and take many crucial steps to get yourself to a better place. First, know that you are loved and wanted in this world. You are strong enough to fight the internal demons. The best way to get to the mental state you want to be in is by healing. Healing looks different for everyone.

"Self-care is how you take your power back." -Lalah Delia

Whether you want to talk to a doctor about medication, see a therapist, open up to someone you love and trust about your past, or however you feel the most comfortable, do it. It will begin your road to recovery and allow you to get your mind to where you desire. Life issues and problems do not stop just because we are feeling depressed. We must take control of our mental health and become strong enough to handle what is thrown in our path.

Living on my own in the new adult world opened my eyes to the importance of mental health. I never thought I needed a counselor or therapist because I felt "fine" and was going through life's regular motions. I suddenly realized that if I were to be in a quiet setting for an extended period of time, my dark and worrying thoughts would overrun my mind. I felt I could not control it when the silence got too loud. When the thoughts crept in, they would scare me.

I could not understand why I would spend hours mindlessly scrolling through social media. Looking back now, it is evident I was using it to avoid the thoughts in my head and distract myself from my battles within. I would lay in bed staring at the ceiling, creating false situations and scenarios that would give me extreme anxiety and stress for no reason. There were a lot of obvious signs that I ignored within my first year of living on my own because I didn't think mental illness applied to me. I noticed a big mood switch when I was on my own. I was sad and depressed for no reason. I had no motivation to accomplish

"You don't have to control your thoughts. You just have to stop letting them control you." -Dan Millman

tasks, even though I had an abundance of work to do. However, I would turn on the "happy switch" when I was around friends. I am sure many of you know how to control your "happy switch" when needed. That itself is scary.

I was unsure why, when I was on my own, I was blanketed in negative thoughts. It took months to understand where I had slipped to and accept that I needed help. In the new year, I made a goal for myself, stating that I would see a counselor or therapist to speak about unspoken issues and past traumas. Forcing myself to be uncomfortable helped immensely in my recovery. I did not think it would work for me or would benefit me in the slightest. But I found that an outsider looking in can identify issues that were not obvious to the everyday perspective.

Ask for help, and know that it is okay to not always be okay. Don't "fake it 'til you make it" because that hurts you even more. Let people see how you genuinely feel so they can help lift you when you need it most.

A lot goes on in the adulting world that affects your mental health negatively and positively. The stress, anxiety, and overwhelming feeling of being independent and making something of your life can impact your mentality.

If you are juggling many life changes simultaneously, it can be challenging for your mind to adjust appropriately. I was the type

"Until you make the unconscious conscious, it will direct your life and you will call it fate." -Carl Jung

of person that would turn to work as a distraction when I became overwhelmed with other situations. I would even use side work to distract me from my daily work issues. I know, not healthy. For a long time, work was my escape from what I felt inside and from other priorities. I let work take over my mental health and bottled my feelings, so I did not have to think about them.

It is easy to get tied up in your first powerful job, as this is your future, and you want to succeed. Working an insane number of hours and using work to mask your feelings can increase the chance of burnout and mental health issues.

Set boundaries for yourself and find a happy medium for work-life balance if you're the type of person to bury yourself in work to avoid your problems. If you do other things to cope with your mental state, such as turning to food, locking yourself away, or anything self-destructive, recognize your actions and seek help when you know you need it. The only person that can truly help and change you is you. If you observe yourself escaping into a dark and dangerous state, find the help that is right for you. Conquering your mental health is learning to eliminate factors that cause you stress, anger, anxiety, depression, and overall destructive emotions. Some of these factors are close to your heart, like family members, old friends, and even social media. The freedom you now hold as someone in the real adult world is quite powerful as you can decide who and what comes and goes in your life. Excluding people and components of your life

> *"What mental health needs is more sunlight, more candor, and more unashamed conversation." – Glenn Close*

that have been with you for a long time is hard. If you notice yourself feeling any repeated negative emotion before, during, or after an interaction with someone, it is time to move on, even if it will be complicated.

Think about what they do or say that puts you in a negative state. Understand that removing pieces or people from your life that are causing significant distress can do a lot of good for you when it comes to your mental health. Now is the time to start over and give yourself a blank slate by considering what makes you stressed and how to remove it from your everyday life. Learn to set safe boundaries for yourself, and only allow people with good intentions and supportive actions and words into your circle. Your environment impacts your mental state. Create a supportive and healing environment through positive people, self-help actions, and a healthy lifestyle.

"Promise me you'll always remember — you're braver than you believe and stronger than you seem, and smarter than you think." -Christopher Robin

Mental Health Check-in

DATE _____

HOW ARE YOU
FEELING THIS WEEK?

HOW ARE YOU
FEELING TODAY?

HOW CAN YOU
IMPROVE YOUR
MENTAL HEALTH?

WHAT HAVE BEEN YOUR
THREE DOMINANT
EMOTIONS THIS WEEK?
○ _____
○ _____
○ _____

WHAT DO YOU FEEL
GOOD ABOUT RIGHT
NOW?

THINGS THAT TRIGGER
NEGATIVE EMOTIONS
○ _____
○ _____
○ _____

MY RANKING OF MY
MENTAL HEALTH THIS
WEEK

☆ ☆ ☆ ☆

Physical Health

This section will not repeat your health class in middle school, explaining that you need to eat fruits and veggies. You know that by now. Instead, this is about taking charge of your physical health as an adult. If you are one of the many college athletes staring retirement in the face, your physical health will never be the same.

Unless you are going pro and competitively continuing your sport, taking care of your health is about to get much more challenging. As an athlete, you have always had your workouts planned for you. Every lifting and cardio session, practice, and game throughout the year was preplanned for the most part during your athletic career.

As you enter your new chapter, you will not have someone telling you exactly what to work out and when to do so. However, if you become successful or get help paying for a personal trainer, you can have a person pushing you to your limits. For most of us, we are on our own when it comes to motivation and workouts. Finding what you like to do to keep yourself active and healthy can be more challenging than you think.

If you have been told for years to lift weights but hate lifting, you do not have to force yourself to do so anymore. There are so many fitness options available; you can do anything that is fun

"Your body holds deep wisdom. Trust in it. Learn from it. Nourish it. Watch your life transform and be healthy." -Bella Bleue

and good for the body. There are so many great options now including hot yoga, HIIT classes, Zumba, pool workouts, and exercise apps that you can easily do at home. Find what you enjoy doing to keep your body in the best shape possible. I encourage you to try one new workout a month. That way, you not only are experiencing a different physical exercise but are practicing an open mindset. If you make it fun and do it with others, you are guaranteed to stick with physical exercise longer.

Balance is critical when prioritizing your physical health. Balance comes in a few different ways. First, find a balance between strenuous and moderate exercise.

You do not need to walk into a gym and decide to rip your muscles apart every single day. If that's what gets you out of bed every day, then go for it—all the power to you. But if you like to have a difficult workout one day and take it easier the next, find that balance and make a schedule that you can easily stick with. Remember that days of rest are needed for the body to recover. Your body needs to refuel and recharge to perform at its peak.

The next part of balancing your physical health is making time for it. As you get wrapped into your new life and job, it is very easy to make excuses and push your physical fitness to the side because you want to focus on everything else happening around you. The working days can get long, decreasing your motivation

"A healthy lifestyle is the most potent medicine at your disposal."
-Sravani Saha Nakhro

to work out. Test out different times of the day to fit in your exercise. See when your body responds best, whether that is early in the morning, during your lunch break, or in the evening to decompress after a long day. Once you find the time of day that works for you, your schedule, and your body, stick to it and remain consistent. Consistency is key to keeping yourself in the shape that you want. If you work hard but also take time to recuperate, your body will be in excellent condition.

Reward yourself for the hard work you put in. For example, I motivate myself to do cardio by allowing myself TV time. I made it a rule that I could only watch my shows while I was doing my inclined walking. That way, I stay on the treadmill longer but also get to "binge" my shows guilt-free. Trust me, I got through my shows a lot faster when I just kept walking and not paying attention to the clock. Develop small, easy ways to keep yourself motivated and focused on your fitness goals.

The last part of balance is food and beverage consumption. We all know we should be fueling ourselves with nutrients and minerals, but sometimes a one-a.m. pizza after a night at the bars sounds irresistible. Let yourself live, and don't force yourself into a diet you know isn't sustainable. My mother always said that she hated the word diet because it has "die" in it. This is exceptionally true because if you have tried going on a diet, you know that you'll start strong but slowly fade out as it becomes more challenging and less appealing. When you limit yourself

"Today is your day to start fresh, to eat right, to train hard, to live healthy, to be proud." -Bonnie Pfiester

and say "don't, can't, won't eat or drink that," your brain does not register those words. It physically cannot comprehend the "don'ts, can'ts, won'ts," making it even harder to sustain a difficult eating and drinking pattern.

Give yourself leeway and freedom to choose to be healthy but also enjoy life's fantastic food and drinks. There are so many incredible places to eat and recipes to make. Why make life dull by limiting yourself to bland food? Be kind to your body and treat it the way you want someone to treat you. We are always our harshest critics, especially when we do not see all the incredible parts of ourselves. Treat yourself with respect and enjoy life's details in a healthy and balanced way.

"It is health that is the real wealth and not pieces of gold and silver."
-Mahatma Gandhi

Let's Grind!
WORKOUT PLANNER

	Activity	Time	Reps
DAY 1			
DAY 2			
DAY 3			
DAY 4			
DAY 5			

CHAPTER 4: DATING

This era of relationships is one for the books. It's a hard pill to swallow, knowing that the hookups, sneaky links, talking stages, and situationships consumed so much time and effort that we cannot get back. The dating world in the twenty-first century can get messy, dirty, secretive, and downright depressing. Finding that person you click with is always the goal, but it feels unachievable when you have been searching for so long.

College sets the tone for this kind of behavior. Think about it: a bunch of teenagers all placed in one area for the first time with freedom. The high sex drives and googly eyes will lead to lots of drama and trouble down the road, as you probably have experienced. Whether you had casual or more serious relationships during your college days, each person you let into your heart (and other places) affected you in some way, good or bad.

You have had time to grow and learn what you truly want in a person. What college fails to prepare you for is the emotional and mental roller coaster of the dating world. You have had to figure it out on your own; unfortunately, it doesn't stop after your diploma is in hand.

Dating outside of college is a whole different ballgame. How? Where do I even begin?

Leaving college with a serious relationship can seem like your

"Dating has taught me what I want and don't want, who I am, and who I want to be." -Jennifer Love Hewitt

entire future is planned out. You both will get jobs, probably move in together after graduating, and begin to settle down to build a life. The "American Dream" sounds nice, but what if your plan crumbles before your eyes?

My story is a messy one. I came out of college dating a guy who I'd been with for nearly three years. After graduation, I decided to move to Dallas, TX to be with him. He felt like the one for me. We had our plan. We would get the jobs we always wanted, live with his parents for a while to save money for a house, and begin building our forever. All was going according to plan, until it wasn't. This fairytale story came collapsing down quickly.

Yes, living with your significant other's parents is a challenge. Every family is different. Values and morals may not be the same, and the household is likely to run differently from your own. Adjusting to someone else's environment can be difficult. However, living with his family was one of the best decisions I made, because it opened my eyes to characteristics and habits I did not like or support.

Two months into my living situation, I knew we would not last. I did not want to face judgment from both sides of the family, knowing I had just uprooted my life for a guy. I was fearful of the backlash I would receive from my family and his. So I stuck it out for a few months, trying to give the relationship a fighting chance to survive, until I got to a point where I could not take the

"You've got to learn to leave the table when love's no longer being served."
-Nina Simone

relationship anymore.

I was scared, felt stuck, and was questioning every decision I had made up to that point because I was about to leave the comfort and familiarity behind and be utterly alone in a brand-new city. I had no friends, no family, and no idea how I would survive on my own.

I broke up with my boyfriend five months after moving in with him. The guy I swore I would marry and start a family with was no longer part of my everyday. I experienced a lot of pain. I was by myself in a big city with no friends and now no support system. I had no idea how I was going to move forward. Life seemed to be ever-changing at a speed that I was incapable of keeping up with.

It was day three after the breakup. I had cried eight times that day. I couldn't make it through a Zoom meeting without breaking down in front of coworkers (humiliating, right)? I was staring into space after work, throwing myself a pity party. Yet, as I lay motionless on the couch, trying to make sense of my life-changing decision, I felt a sense of calm come over me. My mind kept repeating, "New beginning. It's your time."

I sat quietly and listened to my head go back and forth like the devil and the angel. Finally, I mustered up all the energy I had left and pulled myself together. I walked to the bathroom mirror.

"When someone shows you who they are, believe them the first time."
-Maya Angelou

and looked into my pain-filled eyes, and at that moment, I decided to stop. Quit the crying. Quit the pity party. Quit thinking that one dumb boy who didn't fulfill my needs was worth all this heartache.

From that point on, it was about me. I was focusing on a better me. I dug deep into my soul to find that internal motivation to create something memorable. It was my time to shine without anyone or anything holding me back.

There are many lessons to be learned when you completely alter your world. When your gut is telling you that something is not right, listen to it. If you know that a relationship will not last, make the change sooner rather than later. You will save time and stress by eliminating something that does not benefit you. Bottling up the doubt and your true feelings will only worsen the situation. The longer you take to end a relationship that you have been emotionally removed from for a while, the harder it is to continue to live each day like you are "fine." Don't be scared to leave someone or a situation for fear of being alone or regretting it.

You know you best. Make the proper adjustments to make yourself happy, even if you give up comfortability and familiarity. Finding the courage to take charge of your own life and happiness can be tricky, but with the right mindset, you will be in a much better place once you do. Remember why

"It doesn't matter who hurt you or broke you down. What matters is who made you smile again." -Uknown

you are doing what you put yourself through, day in and day out. Consider all your accomplishments to this point and never stop growing.

"You were only meant to be a stepping stone on my journey across the sea."
-Sara Secora

SELF-IMPROVEMENTS

Habits To Change

___

Skills To Learn

___

Values To Enhance

___

Now that you have grown into your fabulous self, you are ready to hit the streets and find that perfect equal. If only it were that easy.

The dating scene post-grad is HARD. Like really hard. First, you must determine what you want from the beginning. When you don't establish your standards for a significant other, you can get caught up in different dating scenes that you might not be comfortable in. If you are looking for some hookups to do some exploring, have that vision established, and let people know ahead of time. Part of growing up is having the courage to tell people what you are precisely looking for. That way, there are no unrealistic expectations.

Ghosting has become all too normal to just about every single person out there. I believe ghosting happens because people are not upfront and honest about what they want in the beginning. People who ghost others also do not have the courage or human decency to let someone know they are no longer interested.

Make it clear about what you want from the beginning to avoid either party getting hurt. Now, I'm not saying come out of the gate stating that you want to marry that person a month after you just met them, but be clear if you are looking for a friends-with-benefits situation, relationship, sneaky link hookup, or anything else. Give each person a chance until they prove they do not deserve one. Go on as many first dates as you want to find

"To the world, you may be one person, but to one person you are the world."
-Unknown

what you like, dislike, and who you will be running away from after that awkward dinner. Doing this will help narrow down exactly what qualities you want in a person.

Be yourself, and enjoy the time spent getting to know other people even if it doesn't work out. Always keep your standards high and never lower them just because you feel someone could be a good fit. I firmly believe that there is no such thing as too high of standards. You deserve someone who will love you unconditionally and always treat you right. If you see red flags in the beginning, run for your life, because you don't want to get stuck in a situation that you could've predicted from the start.

We have all been single at one point in our lives. The exhausting effort of talking to people, getting your hopes up, and being heartbroken is inevitable, even in the old-person world. Dating has become all too digital, with swiping, liking, and DMing, to name a few. The temptation of social media has made dating difficult. Looks are the first parts judged by an admirer, but also, looks can be deceiving. It is easy to make yourself look better with a few quick retouches. Unfortunately, everything you see on social media isn't always natural or authentic, making the dating world more dishonest and cruel.

Let's face it, for a lot of us, dating apps are a never-ending cycle of downloading, swiping, chatting, then deleting. For the lucky ones that find their person on those exhausting apps,

"A person's readiness to date is largely a matter of maturity and environment." -Myles Munroe

I cannot praise you enough, because that is not easy. Apps like Hinge, Tinder, and Bumble are easy and convenient, but think about how many beautiful men and women you see. The pictures do not always match real life; people can pretend to be anyone they want behind the screen. It is a tempting world, and staying committed in just the talking stage is hard for some people to do. Apps have made it easy to become disloyal, treacherous, and emotionally numb to other people and their feelings. Swiping right, swiping left, and trying to come up with cheesy pick-up lines are fun to do for a while, until the revolving disappointment just becomes too mentally exhausting.

Know when to take a break from mindless scrolling. Have enough self-discipline to delete the apps in full and put your efforts into self-improvement when you know you need it. Take time away from trying to get others' attention and validation, and channel that energy towards giving yourself the love you deserve. Improve on any area of yourself. When you invest in yourself and make yourself out to be the person you always dreamed of, that is when things start to fall into place. You become "noticed" even when you believe no one is watching.

Believe it or not, meeting people organically IS possible. It is not an unusual way to meet others, surprisingly. Is it harder? Yes, because it requires you to leave your hermit crab shell and put yourself out there. However, meeting strangers as you go through your daily life is a great way to build a community and

"Dating is something you do before making binding choices or exclusive commitments." -Rebecca Sharp Colmer

connections. You never know whom you might cross paths with just by doing what you enjoy.

When you finally encounter someone who seems worthy of a date and get that awkward small talk out of the way, plan a date that does not involve getting drinks. Drinking is everyone's cop-out, and if you want to see someone's true character, plan an activity rather than sitting and staring at each other, asking the same boring questions. Movement brings out the true character in people and makes time more enjoyable. There is an abundance of easygoing, fun dates that are budget friendly and fun.

Try mini golf, for example. I am atrocious at this game, but it is always nice to laugh about how badly you swing the club. How about a friendly cooking class? Not only do you get to bond over your messy sushi-making skills, but you are putting yourselves out there while showing a bit of vulnerability. Keep dates light and laid back, and don't pressure yourself to make them perfect. Be yourself and let the situation carry itself. Always remember, if it is meant to be, it will be.

As my wise sister once taught me, guard your heart. There will be people out there that will want to use you. It sounds harsh, but some people are just in it for the instant gratification of sex and attention. Be aware of the smooth talkers and love bombers, as they might be in it for one thing and have no intentions of being with you long term. If you are looking for something short term

"I think heartbreak is something that you learn to live with as opposed to learn to forget." -Kate Winslet

then great, go crazy. Keep your incredible heart to yourself until you feel comfortable placing it into other people's hands. You are entrusting them with your emotions and feelings, so be cautious. Having a slight guard up is healthy, especially when meeting new people. Remember to have fun and respect yourself always.

Protecting yourself means cutting off the people that are not providing any value to you. Toxic people, individuals that only call you when they are drunk or lonely, or those that come in and out of your life when they feel like it are negatively affecting you, whether you see it now or in the future. Cutting people like this off can be challenging, because who doesn't want constant affection and validation? A compliment is nice to hear from time to time, even if you know it is a total fuckboy/girl giving it to you, and they have said the same thing to their other ten Tinder matches tonight.

Nonetheless, removing the time-wasters can open doors for others who you might not even know yet exist. People are meant to come into your life for a reason, but that reason might be unknown until long after the relationship ends.

I never believed everyone had a purpose in my life until I experienced a life-changing event. I went on a date with a guy I had started talking to: nothing crazy, just a simple Texas barbecue dinner date. The date was going so well that I decided to skip my recreational volleyball game because I was enjoying

"That's why they call them crushes. If they were easy, they'd call 'em something else." -Sixteen Candles

myself and genuinely interested in him. We ended up being at dinner for over two hours. Afterward, he took me on a walk to show me the area, as I had not been there before. The date went longer than expected, and I had no complaints. I called a friend on the way home, smiling ear to ear because I genuinely enjoyed my time with this guy and knew we would have another date. A second date was a rarity, trust me.

As I slightly sped down the highway home, blabbing away on the phone, I was about to get off at my exit. I glanced to my right and saw a figure standing on the edge of a barricade, barely under the light post. I slammed on my brakes and attempted to pull over immediately, but I was going too fast to stop on the shoulder. I just witnessed a man getting ready to jump to his death on the road below him.

I frantically hung up the phone with my friend and called 911. My distraught and anxious brain attempted to give them the approximate location of where this man was standing. I had to circle back on the highway to try and get to him before he took action, but I had no idea if I was going to reach him in time or even if the police would. I was scared and fearful that this man would act upon his thoughts before someone could help him. Within a minute and a half, the operator put me on hold and shortly came back to let me know that the officers had taken him down from the barricade. I had just returned onto the highway and could pass by and see the man myself. He was

"Life is the first gift, love is the second, and understanding the third."
-Marge Piercy

sitting down on the shoulder of the road, head hanging low, with a look of defeat and sadness on his face. Four police officers had him handcuffed and held by the arm, talking with him. The relief I felt was incredible, knowing that this man would live to see another day.

How does the story relate to why people come into your life? I was not supposed to be driving home at this time of night. I skipped my volleyball game to stay for the date, and the date lasted longer than the game would have. If I had cut off the date and gone to volleyball, I would've missed the man looking to his death. I believe the guy I went out with was put into my life so that I could save another.

Understanding that every person has a reason why they come into my life took a long time to accept, because this guy and I went out a few more times, and I developed feelings for him. He was the first guy I had felt something for since my breakup. He seemed perfect for me, and I couldn't understand why it wasn't meant to be.

As I had my minor breakdown after going our separate ways, I realized that he was placed in my life for a short time so that the man on the highway could live and receive help. It cut deep, but I would rather be sad over a short situationship than someone losing their life.

"Love is shown more in deeds than in words." -Saint Ignatius

So, I challenge you to think deeper about why people are placed in your life. The *why* just might surprise you.

"You meet thousands of people and none of them really touch you. And then you meet one person and your life is changed forever." -Love & Other Drugs

YOUR WHYS

People, good and bad, have a reason for coming into our life. Think about some people that have made an impact on your life at any point. What did they teach you? Why were they around during a specific time period? What have you provided for them? Fill this out to help you see the deeper meaning of life's interactions.

NAME: WHY:

In the dating world after college, you might feel the need to lower your standards or accept behavior that you wouldn't typically just so that you have someone to fill that missing piece. Becoming desperate to have companionship can cause people to settle for someone who is not suitable for them. I learned about settling when I entered the cold-hearted dating world. I thought everyone had good intentions when dating others. I was quickly humbled.

We long for that instant connection with someone, causing us to proceed with relationships even if we know they are not in our best interest.

Forcing a connection and a relationship in the beginning only sets you up for failure in the future. It's hard to overcome all the hurt and loss you have dealt with in your love life and raise your standards to where you know they should be. However, suppose you consistently practice looking for red flags in behavior and habits that you would never accept in the very early stages of dating. In that case, it will set the standards for all your relationships to come.

Everyone always told me never to compromise my values for anybody when I was dating, no matter how they spoke to me or what they did for me. Those sweet talkers and insincere gestures can really influence you to think that this person is interested in you. Sincerity is gone in this world because people say what others want to hear to fulfill their needs at that given time.

"Our soulmate is the one who makes life come to life." -Richard Bach

People have become untrustworthy, and the more heartbreak you feel, the less you trust anyone with your heart. Values have become a distant thought as many people drop what they believe to lower their standards for someone else. I fell victim to letting go of my values when I entered the dating world.

I was twenty-two and single. I had not been single since the age of fifteen, so I honestly did not know how to act or what to expect. No one prepared me for all the toxic parts of dating. In the long run, I lost myself for a while. I lost respect for my body, my heart, and my time. I accepted behavior that I would never tolerate if I were thinking straight.

Some men used me for attention, time, and physical intimacy, but in my head, I thought this was normal, and I let them. Through the pain and hurt, I realized that I had been wrapped up in a dating world fairyland where I thought it was entertaining, but it was damaging to the heart and soul. The attention from guys kept me hooked for a lot longer than it should have. I did not look for red flags and ignored behaviors that I wouldn't usually accept.

My actions showed my immaturity. I thought the guys I went out with wanted to be with me, but in reality, they wanted their quick fix of dopamine and female validation. We can all admit that the attention you get in the dating world is nice. Good-looking people saying you are sexy, hot, cute, beautiful,

"Don't look for a partner who is eye candy. Look for a partner who is soul food." -Karen Salmansohn

handsome, etc., is a nice ego boost. But, after a while, the constant empty compliments get old because you have heard them repeatedly, eventually leading to those words meaning nothing.

Unfulfilling words lead to never accepting a compliment because you begin to believe everyone is faking it to get your attention or something out of you. I felt degraded because guys truly only wanted what was on the outside and did not try to get to know the true me on the inside. I wished guys would see past my body to who I am on the inside. I wished they would've seen my success so young in life, my personality, and my large heart for others. I couldn't understand why no one wanted to know the true me. It was months after I started dating when I realized that I had given them just enough of what they wanted, so they did not feel the need to get to know me. This summary of myself is not something I am proud of, and I will be the first to admit it hurt a bit. I would lay myself out there initially and give them everything in the beginning in hopes that I was exactly what each guy was looking for in a girlfriend.

What do you know? I was not. If I had kept my core values close to my heart and recognized red flags from the beginning, I would have avoided a lot of hurt and disappointment along the way.

Even though the dating world can be miserable, no Prince Charming will knock on your door one random night, coming

"If you wished to be loved, love." -Lucius Annaeus Seneca

to take you away by horse into the sunset. Meeting someone takes time and putting yourself out there as much as possible. We have all heard that soulmates come when you're not looking or least expect it. If you are constantly on the prowl, attempting to find the next person to Netflix and chill with, you are only filling the void of not having a person. You are not seeking one particular person. It will come with time, patience, and trust in yourself and the process.

When people told me I had to wait for that special someone, it would drive me insane. What do you mean that I have to wait? As an impatient person, this did not sit well with me. I learned that if I took the process slower, I would not initially give up so much of myself. Instead, I would learn about someone and give them time to get to know me. If someone is serious about getting to know you, the sex and physical aspects of the relationship can wait. Someone with your best interests at heart will not lead you to the bedroom. Instead, the right one will lead you to experience a better version of yourself.

They will lift you up and encourage you to become the best you can be. It is hard to go slow when you're very excited about someone, but take things slow. Do not give someone a total rundown of your life from the beginning. Attention spans are shorter today, and many people get "bored" if they already know everything about someone up front. Stay reserved enough to protect yourself and your heart, but give pieces of your life that

"Your soulmate will be the stranger you recognize." -r.h. Sin

you feel are worth sharing. If they want to get to know you, they will try to do so as time goes on. If you lay it all out in the beginning, it could hurt your chances of actually ending up with that person. Keep yourself grounded and level-headed by slowly opening up and showing your true colors as you feel a bond forming. Gradually become comfortable with the person and have open and honest conversations about what you want from them.

Since we were young, we have received lessons on self-respect. For middle school-aged students, this subject doesn't exactly scream excitement. I remember everyone rolling their eyes at the topic because everyone thought, *"Who doesn't respect themselves?"* Even if you say you respect yourself, your actions will reflect if you genuinely do.

Low self-respect leads you to make decisions you wouldn't usually make and accept toxic behavior that can damage you. For example, when someone experiences much rejection in the dating world, we often think that lowering our expectations is how we will attract the person we are looking for because we feel "too picky."

I am here to tell you that pickiness is suitable for dating. Being picky about whom you spend your time with and give your heart to is essential. It means you respect yourself enough to wait for the right person to treat you well. You are worthy of

"Date someone who is home and an adventure all at once." -Unknown

a healthy, strong relationship with someone who will show up daily for you. If I learned anything during my tough dating life post-college, never settle for mediocre people. They will not treat you like you deserve to be treated.

When dating, it is essential to evaluate where you stand with yourself. What I mean is, what stage are you currently in? Are you looking for hookups to test the waters and see what you like and don't like? Are you searching for something more serious and wanting to take things slow with people you go out with? Regardless of your stage, constantly check up on yourself to ensure you do what is right for you.

If you feel you will regret doing something, don't follow through with it, and know it is okay to move on to the next person or situation. I noticed myself struggling to let go of people even though I knew they were terrible for me. Almost every guy I went out with I regret because I knew they were not it for me.

I let my morals and guard down, leading me to make decisions that left me empty and depressed. I did not set boundaries and expectations early on, causing me to fall out of character and into a place I was not comfortable in.

I thought going out with many guys was the trick to finding my next soul mate, but in reality, I did not have an honest conversation about what I was looking for with myself.

"We cannot really love anyone with whom we never laugh." -Agnes Repplier

My actions hurt my self-respect, and I had to reflect on my own to see why I was acting this way, what could be done to fix this behavior, and what my standards should be. I realized that I wanted to slow down the talking stage process and really try to get to know someone before I went out with them. I worked on looking for red flags early on so I could decide whether or not to give my time to someone that genuinely deserved it.

Never compromise your standards, expectations, and interests to appeal to one person or make someone look more appealing than they are. Red flags are an actual piece of dating; the more you recognize them in the beginning, the more likely you will stick to your standards. You deserve more than what you think you do.

Finding the right one can be daunting, but your twenties are meant for learning how to navigate relationships based on your experiences. You might go through quite a few failed talking stages before you find the right person. But understand your person is out there, and someone is waiting to treat you the way you deserve to be treated.

If you are lucky and have found the person placed on this earth for you, be the best partner you can be with them. Grow together, learn together, and never stop loving each other!

Take a moment to fill out the next page and talk about what your standards are for a partner.

"The best and most beautiful things in this world cannot be seen or even heard —they must be felt with the heart." -Helen Keller

Relationship Standards

You deserve the world and more. Write down your expectations and standards when looking for a partner. Never settle for less!

Safety While Dating

Netflix murder documentaries have scarred me for life, so we will discuss keeping yourself safe while dating. While the world has incredible people with big hearts, there are a few scary people. When you are active on dating sites, use your first name only and generic photos of yourself. Keeping yourself "mysterious" will make it a little harder for someone to find your entire life story on the internet.

You probably know this by now, but the general rule is that when you first go out with someone, meet in public places for a while until you feel more comfortable with the person. Always let someone know where you will be, or better yet, share your location with friends or family so they know where you are always. College made it easy to date because the campus is generally a safe space, so you trust people more. The outside world is not as trustworthy, so always watch for unusual behavior or speech. If a date is joking about roofying a drink at happy hour, maybe keep an extra-close watch on what you are consuming and keep that in mind if you think you might want to see them again. Dangerous individuals drop subtle hints without realizing it. Never share the exact location of where you live and other specific areas that you frequent. If you ever feel unsafe, make an excuse to leave early and take a different route home than normal to ensure someone is not following you. Keeping yourself will protect you from the creeps out there.

"You meet thousands of people and none of them really touch you. And then you meet one person and your life is changed forever." -Love & Other Drugs

Loneliness

This last topic of dating is often forgotten about. I am going to put it bluntly and honestly. Nothing has prepared you for the loneliness you will feel while looking for a serious relationship. It is the cold, hard truth. Being single and working on yourself while trying to find someone at your level is a solitary process. There are nights when all you want to do is cuddle with someone that cares about you, but you simply can't. I will say this. Being in the arms of someone who truly loves you is much more fulfilling than hitting up a past fling to have an empty physical presence. The painfully quiet and long nights strengthen you, and when you finally find that person, the time waiting becomes worth it.

You might have already discovered this, but in post-grad life, you are not surrounded by hundreds of people daily, which changes your perspective of loneliness. If you want social interaction and a dating life, you must force yourself to go out and meet people. This challenging and daunting task takes a lot of time and effort. For example, going on lots of dates in a short amount of time can be fun for a while because you are meeting new people and starting new conversations. However, as many of you probably know, it gets old quickly. It becomes repetitive and unproductive if you are not focusing on forming genuine connections and just meeting a bunch of people at a surface level. The mindless swiping, worthless messaging, empty conversations and

"Imagine meeting someone who even understood the dustiest corners of your mixed-up soul." -Unknown

the feeling of not being wanted consumes your thoughts once the dating apps have lived out their life. You could be messaging five different people, yet feel so alone at the same time. There isn't much depth in the relationships, leaving you feeling emptier and more hopeless.

I had no idea what dating apps consisted of. I quickly learned that many people say what they think you want to hear to get your attention, but really the words mean nothing. I thought all the attention would help me feel less lonely because it felt like multiple people cared about me when, they didn't. After one failed talking stage after another, I felt that no one would truly want me. Loneliness came over me in every setting I put myself in. Whether I was alone in my apartment, at a crowded bar, or even hanging out with friends, I felt alone just because I didn't have someone loving me.

It took nearly a year to come to terms with "singleness." I describe it as being okay with being alone. I had never experienced this before, but as I gathered myself out of a dark hole, I realized it was okay to be on my own right now. Now is the time of life when you can be selfish and do whatever you want without worrying about others. Being single shouldn't be a sad or lonely state. Instead, it should be a time to reflect on yourself and improve in areas of your life that you wish to work on. Of course, it is good to date occasionally, but focusing on yourself attracts some of the best people to your life.

"Important encounters are planned by the souls long before the bodies see each other." -Paulo Coelho

Picture this. You are sitting in a restaurant, staring at the empty chair in front of you. As you scan the room to see who might be judging you (no one really is, I promise), you shovel bites of food into your mouth, hoping you aren't making a fool of yourself. Then, you lock eyes again with that empty chair across from you. Think about it. Would you rather be eating on your own, enjoying yourself, or eating across from someone who doesn't make you happy? How much would you be enjoying that meal if that chair was filled with someone who did not support you, was not loyal to you, and wasn't your person?

That empty chair should remain open until the right person arrives in your life. Think about how good it will feel one day when that chair is taken by someone that looks at you as if you are the only person in the room. You will eat thousands of meals with this particular person. Don't let your loneliness persuade your judgment on someone causing you to settle for someone that doesn't deserve you. Your happiness, well-being, and quality of life matter much more than bragging to your friends on Instagram that you are engaged to someone you don't love. Your person will come. Rushing to fill the pieces of your life that seem "empty" will only lead to poor decisions. It is not a good recipe for a prosperous life, and it will only harm you in the long run.

Burying your head into your phone, work, or other distractions is not the answer to fixing your loneliness. Distracting yourself and finding instant gratification through social media, dating apps, or

"There are no accidental meetings between souls." -Sheila Burke

any other form of entertainment only shields your feelings. Instead, be present with yourself, your emotions, and how you respond to your environment. When you are doing activities alone, keep your phone down. You will appear more approachable and carry a confidence that others will notice. Keep your head up and show people how strong of a person you are. Become the best version of yourself you possibly can and watch the pieces of your life fall into place.

"You had me at hello." -Jerry McGuire

CHAPTER 5: FRIENDSHIPS

Starting over with brand-new people is quite difficult. You have to make an effort to go out and meet people. You aren't in this protective college bubble that gives you all the options in the world for friends. Once you step out of college fairytale land, people will come and go out of your life. If you are looking for a total reset, finding new people to spend time with can be exhausting but rewarding when you find the right individuals.

If you choose to move back home where you know people from your childhood, that is great. It is comfortable, and there is history there. It is nice to have people that know you from an early stage of life; however, it is crucial to begin your new life with new people, too. It will allow you to break out of your comfort zone and find other people like you. Surround yourself with individuals with new perspectives and different personalities than you are used to. Variety in friendships creates a flourishing environment for yourself.

I am not saying to cut out the people that have been there for you since day one. However, you are getting older as time passes (yes, not that old, but still, time is ticking), meaning you should be pickier with the people you choose to spend your time with. Your time is valuable, and you should treat it that way.

Spend time with the friends in your life who bring positivity, value, and happiness, and discard the ones that don't. That may seem harsh, but think about how your mood changes when you

"Find a group of people who challenge and inspire you; spend a lot of time with them, and it will change your life." -Amy Poehler

are with a negative person or someone that always shoots you down. They do not provide any respect or honor to your life, so why keep them around?

When you are with people who are dragging you down, unsupportive of your goals, and stuck reliving the past, it will only hinder your potential and not allow you to grow as a person. Blurring the lines between your new and old life as a teenager can be confusing. That is why having high-quality friends who support your growth is so important.

Finding friends with similar interests and who support your decisions in life will make a difference in your day-to-day routine. Starting new friendships can be difficult. You might feel like you must act like someone you're not in order to fit in with anyone because you long to be liked by others. Never compromise your true self to try and fit in with peers. Know what you can bring to the table and keep your standards high, even in friendships. Know that if friendships are not meeting your needs or matching your criteria, it is better to be alone than suffer through a relationship that brings no benefit to you in the long run. Good friends should provide support and happiness, bringing out the best version of you.

As the years go on, I feel that finding genuine people is almost impossible. Pure people are hard to come by because of the ways we now interact with one another in the digital age.

> *"Time doesn't take away from friendship, nor does separation."*
> *-Tennessee Williams*

So if you have found those rare gems of people, keep them around. If you are still looking, you might wonder how you find them.

Believe it or not, there are quite a few activities for young adults looking to meet friends. Many larger cities have sports and social clubs to join that include all interests. Joining groups you like is a great way to let loose and have fun with others. You can laugh at your mistakes and keep a light heart while enjoying being active. Letting yourself become vulnerable through activities and groups is an excellent way to find common ground with others and put yourself out there.

Are sports not your thing? There are many art classes, acting groups, and interest groups to join. Try an app like MeetUp, where you join groups of people with similar interests. Many happy hours, game nights, and event gatherings happen daily. Get out of your comfort zone and find others with similar interests. It is a good starting point that can later lead to a great foundation. Attending new events allows you to meet different people to see whom you want to start building solid relationships with outside of your common interest. And who knows, you might even meet someone special.

If you want to meet people for a coffee date or a walk in the park, apps like BumbleBFF can help you find people in the same situation. If you feel lonely, try this and see what the

"Don't make friends who are comfortable to be with. Make friends who will force you to lever yourself up." -Thomas J. Watson

swiping game brings to the table. You have nothing to lose; you might as well try it out. But, of course, the section about safety applies to this as well!

Once you find others with similar interests and build good friendship connections, you can begin to grow with others in your new stage of life. Going out to bars and clubs together is fun, but hang out sober to ensure you actually like their presence. It might sound like a funny idea, but many people fall into the trap of only hanging out with new friends when alcohol or other substances are involved. When you hang out with people sober, you can see their true character and decide whether to continue to be around them or not. You have had plenty of experience making friends by this point in life. You know when someone is toxic, and the best thing you can do is acknowledge these behaviors from the beginning and cut them off once you notice the red flags. You are beginning your next phase of life. The last thing you need is drama and people holding you back.

People come into your life for a reason or a season. If a new friend does not work out, understand that there is probably a lesson to be learned from being around that person. People that do not have your best interests at heart are not worth your time. Friendship should always be 50/50, and the effort should be equal. Be picky about who you spend your days with as you begin to adapt to the habits and lifestyle you choose.

"Everyone you meet knows something you don't know but need to know. Learn from them." -C.G. Jung

Finding new people to hang out with is exciting. The adventures, conversations, and thrills are captivating. It is hard to pass up a happy hour, night out, or a weekend getaway with new people because fear of missing out is a natural feeling. It is more than okay to spend a reasonable amount of time with friends, but find a balance between friends and alone time. Sometimes too much togetherness can lead to resentment and irritation with a friend. Give yourself an environment in which you can thrive on your own. Space is necessary to better yourself and improve upon your goals. Learning to succeed on your own is essential to growing as an individual.

The more you better yourself, the more your relationships and friendships will flourish. Prioritize yourself in every situation and make the best decisions that will benefit you in the long run.

"Anything is possible when you have the right people there to support you."
-Misty Copeland

Friendship Bingo

Every friendship is a two-way street. Mark in one color something you want in a friend. Use a different color to mark what you provide as a friend. If one is split, use both colors!

communication	clairvoyance	respect	tough love	helpfulness
integrity	goals and ambitions	reciprocal effort	acceptance	genuineness
dependability	support	*Free*	patience	resilience
empathy	provider of joy	loyal	forgiveness	humor
listens with intent	contagious positivity	self-confidence	courage	soul mate

Partying

Long live the college party life. It is legendary. There is no other time of your life where drinking five days a week with two blackouts is genuinely acceptable, except for college. The memorable game days that made weekends magical will forever burn in your mind. You know those unforgettable parties and humorous moments I am talking about. And the best feeling is being able to shred that fake I.D. and not have an anxiety attack every time you encounter a bouncer.

The fun can continue in the adult world whether you partied only a little bit or too much in college. If you so choose, the party life can remain the same or even get crazier. Yes, somehow, that is possible.

Life is about balance, and partying is no exception. Your choices can affect you long-term and short-term, even after college. With the world at your disposal, trying every bar in the city might seem like a good idea. However, I learned the hard way that self-control is essential. The bars will always be there, but money, time, and energy won't always be available. If you wish to try different places, set aside a certain amount of money each month to allocate towards that fun, and stick to it. That way, you can have fun without blowing your entire paycheck on expensive drinks.

"A true friend never gets in your way unless you happen to be going down."
-Arnold H. Glasgow

Making friends is challenging, as we have already discussed, but as a post-grad adult, a great way to meet people is at bars. That slick alcohol makes everyone more talkative, and it's the extra nudge people need to talk to strangers. However, making smart decisions is key with so many options and places to go. Make sure you are being safe and aware of your surroundings at all times. Try to connect with individuals who might have the same interests and are easygoing. You never know what connection you might make!

Let's say you want to take a leap of faith and go out by yourself. Going to bars on your own can be intimidating. It is hard not to bury your nose in your phone, pretending that you have people to text and apps to scroll through when you are alone in a social setting. My best advice is to avoid doing this as much as possible to make yourself present in the moment. You will look more inviting when people glance your way.

If you choose to go out alone, pick a more relaxed environment where conversations are effortless. Confidence is essential, and a friendly, warm smile is always an excellent invitation for someone to approach you. If you are brave, start a conversation with the person next to you. It can't hurt. Conversation with strangers can be intriguing, but sitting back and people-watching from your seat is also a great way to pass some time and get out in a social environment. Relax and enjoy yourself. Life is too short to worry about being somewhere alone.

"Every new friend is a new adventure... the start of more memories."
-Patrick Lindsay

If you enjoy going out with friends, take the time to experience new places together. Everyone will be curious about the undiscovered spot, so it takes the edge off a bit. If they are new friends, be cautious about how much you drink the first few times you go out. You will want to make sure that they are safe to be around when you are intoxicated. Read the personalities, situations, and environment to ensure these people can be trusted. Establishing trust with friends when sober and intoxicated will help set a solid foundation, and you will know if they are genuine people.

Going out with friends to bars, clubs, and local hangouts is fun, but it also can be mentally and physically exhausting. If you notice yourself slipping emotionally, mentally, or even in your work, take a step back and take a break. "Party breaks" are necessary to keep yourself in check. Your body and mind are not meant to handle a lot of late nights and dehydrated mornings. If there is a weekend when you just want to chill, don't feel bad telling your friends you want to stay in. If they are true friends, they will tell you to enjoy your time or even ask to join you on a chill night. Never let yourself get pressured to go out just because it is the "cool" thing to do. No bar or club is worth sacrificing your health. Take time for yourself and listen to your body and wallet. Let's face it: going out can be damaging to the financials.

"A friend can tell you things you don't want to tell yourself."
-Frances Ward Weller

This or That

Mark your preferences and write down which places and/or things you want to try! Then, make it a goal to hit one of these monthly to keep life exciting.

Dive Bars OR Upscale Bars
_____   _____
_____   _____
_____   _____

Nightclubs OR Outdoor Bars
_____   _____
_____   _____
_____   _____

New Experiences OR New Drinks
_____   _____
_____   _____
_____   _____

New Restaurants OR New Recipes
_____   _____
_____   _____
_____   _____

Loud Environment OR Quiet Environment
_____   _____
_____   _____
_____   _____

With Friends OR Alone
_____   _____
_____   _____
_____   _____

CHAPTER 6: SUPPORT SYSTEM

You are turning into an independent boss who is killing it in life. You're living on your own, making significant decisions without anyone standing in your way. The big world can get to your head quickly, which, at times, is okay. However, just because you are on your own doesn't mean you must remove everyone from the past altogether. There will be rough patches in the adult world where you need someone to lean on. The people who have supported you are the reason why you have gotten to where you are today.

When you are out doing your own thing, focusing on chasing your dreams and creating a new life, quality time with the people that matter most can slip through the cracks. You are older now, but so is everyone else around you. As you grow into your adult self these next few years, time goes by faster than ever. It is scary to watch life fly by, and you might not even notice it. Time is uncontrollable, and we only have so much until the people we care about aren't with us anymore.

The hustle and bustle of the daily grind can be exhausting. You have to keep up with many different demands from work, home chores, and navigating a new life. Picking up the phone and calling your favorite aunt doesn't always cross your mind. This point in life is when it matters most. When you visit family and friends or even FaceTime them, it means even more now. It means you're taking time out of your personal life that you have created and want to spend time with them.

"Support and encouragement are found in the most unlikely places."
-Raquel Cepeda

You're showing your love and affection for those people by giving them the attention they deserve.

It is easy to be selfish and forget about calling and maintaining those relationships you've left behind that are still important. Make an effort to speak to those who built you up the most and made the most significant positive impact in your life. They raised you to be who you are today and supported everything you wanted. They will not be around forever, and you never want to regret not calling them or not checking in on them when you know you should've. Your life will be there, but those people won't always be.

Moving away taught me how important my support system was. I am very lucky to say my family and closest friends were my biggest support systems. They provided me with guidance, advice, a shoulder to cry on, an ear to rant to and a whole lot of love and support. Every person that is close to me provided different support than the next. I would call my grandparents at least once a week to talk about everyday life and keep them updated on what was going on. I talked to my parents frequently to get advice on adult things, because adulting is hard! My friends listened as I broke down after breakups and failed relationships. They picked me up when I wasn't strong enough to do it for myself. They showed me how blessed I am to have the life that I live and assured me there was a light at the end of every dark tunnel. The outpouring of affection from all the different

"The moment you accept that there's a guidance system supporting you, then you experience a new sense of freedom and peace." -Gabrielle Bernstein

people in my life allowed me to believe in myself and live the life that I was destined for. I would not be where I am today without each and every one of them.

If you are religious, this can also help guide you through your adult life. I learned that leaning on my faith, God and scripture helped me get through my darkest times. I had been removed from my faith for a few years but as I spent many lonely nights laying in bed, I knew I could always talk to God and read scripture to help me find peace before sleeping. I would thank Him for the good things in life but also cry to Him about the struggles I was going through. I found great healing from practicing my faith more as I navigated the daily situations I faced.

Your faith can never be taken away from you. Embrace what you believe in and allow your heart to open up. You will grow as an individual if you continually count on your beliefs and the positive people in your life.

"You can't live entirely alone. You need some kind of a support system."
-Wendall Berry

Stay in Touch

Keep track of the people you wish to contact on a regular basis. Write their name and how often you will keep in touch with them.

Family	Business Contacts

Organizations	Friends

CHAPTER 7: COMMUNICATION

Why is communication in this book? Well, I realized how much our generation lacks connecting with others through words. Our faces are constantly buried in our screens, and we have learned the behavior of avoiding conversation when things get complicated.

I want to talk about the importance of excellent communication. Some of you might have grown up in a home where healthy conversation was a foreign concept. Others might have been in toxic relationships with family, friends, and significant others where communicating was impossible. Then, somewhere down the line, someone made us feel that we could not talk about how we felt, our expectations, or the issues going on in life.

Feeling like you are not heard or listened to is one of the most belittling feelings. You feel your voice getting softer, and you are screaming for someone to listen to you, but no one does.

The more beat down you get, the more resentment you will have towards that person that won't give you the time of day. Maturing is realizing who the people are in your life that make it hard to have an open dialogue. When you accept that the person may never change and you might not be able to communicate with them entirely, that is when you begin to limit your time with those individuals. Toxic environments deplete your growth.

We all deserve to protect our peace and have healthy, stable

"Wise men speak because they have something to say; Fools because they have to say something." -Unknown

relationships with good communication. Strong friendships, relationships, and family bonds begin with good conversation. You should have a safe space to talk about your struggles, what is going on in life, and how someone is affecting you.

I always thought I was a good communicator. I would tell people how I felt, whether they wanted to hear it or not. I was blunt, honest, and probably a bit mean because I did not have a strong filter. During my teenage years, I could be a very angry individual. I lashed out a lot at my family, and definitely could be a bad friend at times. I was explosive with my emotions. If something was making me mad, I would scream and yell at times. My words were hurtful and destructive to others. I had no control over the words exiting my mouth. My extreme reactions were from bottled-up emotions and an inability to communicate them appropriately.

During college, I discovered how my behavior and lack of maturity in communication truly affected the relationships I left back in Denver. Once I was in college, my relationship with my parents improved significantly because I had the space to digest information and think before losing my cool on them.

My friendships at home dwindled after my freshman year of college. My high school boyfriend and I broke up, and it was ugly. I was very bitter and angry, and the result of that was some nasty behavior. I lost all of my high school friends because

"Much unhappiness has come into the world because of bewilderment and things left unsaid." -Fyodor Dostoevsky

I was too immature to talk about how badly the breakup affected me. I felt sides were taken, and there was no room left for me in the group. I often think about what could have been if it were not for my actions, but I had to move on and learn from my mistakes. Unfortunately, I did not communicate how it made me feel and didn't take action to make the best of the situation to keep the friends I did have.

As I grew through college, I knew I had a short fuse. It was more evident when I got irritated, annoyed, and furious. I had little patience for people who weren't doing things as I thought they should. At this point in my life, I was aware of how my communication, or lack thereof, could get out of hand. I would sometimes get angry with my college boyfriend or a friend. I was not consciously working on my patience or understanding of how others might feel.

Fast forward to post-college. I am attempting to make friends and find someone to create a forever with, and communication is a crucial piece to being able to connect people. I had to work on my habits of speaking. I had to become more understanding and more gentle towards others, but also trust these new people with my feelings as I was going through the most challenging part of my life. The way my sweet friends comforted me and were there for me in my darkest hours was so inspiring. They allowed me to have a safe space to let out all my emotions, picked me up, and helped me go on with life.

"One of the most important things you can do on this earth is to let people know they are not alone." -Shannon L. Alder

It took getting to the lowest low to realize how much I needed to communicate differently. After that, I slowly learned how to improve my actions and words. Since then, I am much more cognisant of my words, my tone, and how my words could greatly impact someone. Ten years before, I would've said anything to someone even if I knew it was extremely mean to say.

I worked on speaking to my family more nicely and softly, being more tolerant of how others process emotions and situations, and providing a safe environment for my friends to come to me when they are hurting. I wanted open dialogue with everyone close to me so they felt heard and so I could too. Amazingly, my friendships and family bonds all improved significantly as I worked on emotional maturity.

I have accepted how my old self was in romantic relationships and actively improved my patience, and created a better environment for me and the man I am with to have a safe space to talk about our relationship. As a result, I would tell the guy I was seeing what I was looking for and what my intentions were upfront. I also did check-ins periodically to ensure both parties got what they needed out of the relationship and that each person was heard.

There is no time frame for improving communication. As you can see, it took me YEARS to finally grasp what healthy dialogue

"Words are, of course, the most powerful drug used by mankind."
-Rudyard Kipling

consisted of. It is not an easy road to endure, but when you decide to connect with others on a deeper level, communication is the only way to go. If you can sit back and reflect on family, friends, and romantic relationships and understand where you can improve, I promise you will blossom into a good communicator. Work on it daily, and others will notice the slow improvements. Use your words in more face-to-face interactions to work on your conversation skills. Process words and emotions slower to truly understand your feelings and what to share. The more you think about your words, the better conversations you will have.

If someone close to you is not good with words, help and guide them to a safe place so they can become more comfortable with the environment of sharing their thoughts with you. Improving all of your conversations to healthy ones will be an excellent foundation for life moving forward. When you learn to correctly communicate your thoughts and feelings, you will change for the better as an individual.

"But good healthy communication is impossible without openness, honesty, and vulnerability." -Paul Kendall

Improved Words

We need to practice using our words wisely and being good communicators. Think about different situations, how you felt, and how communication could be improved.

SITUATION 1

SITUATION 2

SITUATION 3

SITUATION 4

CHAPTER 8: CAREER

The idea of a career has been altered significantly since our parents were in school. Back then, it was tradition to go to college, get a degree that you half-cared about, get out and do something within that path. If you strayed from this preplanned path, you were seen as "crazy" or "risky." These "risks" helped build the mindset for the generations to come. These people helped develop the world into what it is today.

Think about how you determined what degree you would get. It was based on something you liked, something intriguing to you, or it was downright forced upon you. You have dedicated years of your life to studying this subject. School might have taught you some things, but your research and experience are most likely more valuable. Your degree doesn't teach you how to build and grow in your career field. It only gives you a piece of paper to get your butt in the door. Your experience, soft skills, and knowledge get you farther. Since you have nearly completed this track, how will you fully maximize your potential with this expensive piece of paper in your pocket?

Since I was young, I have been an organized, ambitious person who likes to be the boss. Because of my personality traits, I wanted to enter the event-planning industry. This fast-paced, think-on-your-feet, plan-ahead life sounded perfect to me. So I chose a school that offered a degree in event planning. I was happy and excited but unsure what direction to go after college. Planning weddings was not on my radar, as I would not

"The future depends on what you do today." -Mahatma Gandhi

want to deal with bridezillas daily. I was going to take my time and figure out what industry suits my skills best. Three months into college, I was sitting in my advisor's office, looking to plan classes for the following semester. We sat down and looked for the degree program's class layout sheet. My advisor and I started to search for this page. We sifted through every building's catalog, website, and even physical copies of degrees.

My advisor asked fellow professors if they had heard of this degree or even seen the course schedule. Each one looked at us strangely and shook their heads. Panic started to set in. After researching the entire university and asking every dean involved, we found that there was a mistake. The degree program I chose did not even exist yet. It was on the university website but was not going to be approved until two years later. My anxiety soared, sending my heart rate through the roof and my mind spinning with panicked thoughts.

How was this even possible? I picked a school 1,000 miles from home for a degree program that did not even exist. Event planning was my passion, and I was ecstatic to have a career in the industry. To make matters worse, a dean of the business school said that the degree program was still pending approval, meaning there was a chance it would never be available. I now realize that the entire direction I chose did not exist there and had a chance of never existing. In a matter of minutes, I had no idea what I wanted to do with my life. My entire track got derailed,

"If you want to achieve greatness, stop asking for permission." -Eddie Colla

and I couldn't do anything to fix it.

I walked out of my advisor's office in a daze. I was nineteen years old, being told that I came to a college far away for basically nothing. I took about a week to gather my thoughts and discuss my situation with friends and family. I needed all my opinions and advice because I was like a lost puppy.

I took some time to think about what I wanted in life. After calming myself down and creating an open mind, I met with my advisor again. He could tell I was on edge and scared about my track at the university. He calmly mentioned that marketing is very similar to event planning. Marketing was a different strategy for a brand, but still significant. He stated that with my personality and mindset, this might be an excellent interim degree to accomplish while I wait for the one I wanted to be approved.

I had nothing else to go for, so I said *Fuck it* and signed up for a Bachelor of Arts in Marketing degree. This last-minute, gut-wrenching decision turned out to be one of the best choices I ever made during my time in school.

Not surprisingly, I fell in love with the marketing world and decided I did not want to do event planning anymore. My eyes were opened by the opportunities available in the big-girl world. There was a lot there for me to excel in and learn about. This career path fits me better than the original plan. I was ready to

"Work hard in silence, let your success be your noise." -Frank Ocean

take on life ahead.

Change happens on a flip of a dime. What you are interested in when you are eighteen years old is much different when the big twenty-one rolls around. Changing your path in life is okay. Seriously, you can change your mind a hundred times, which is normal. Your tastes, interests, and personality all change drastically during those four years at college.

Many of you are coming out of your senior year with the idea that you might not want to do what you thought. Now is the time to embrace it and write your story.

The best part is that most people do not even use their degrees anymore or go on a similar career path. Life has exciting twists and turns when it comes to a career.

Newsflash: you do not have to have your next five years planned out to a tee before you strut your stuff across that stage. If you are approaching the end of your glorious college career and you still don't have a job lined up because you don't know what to do, good. Stay picky and open-minded. The internet gives us many ways to make a living through remote work and side hustles. Take time for yourself and test the waters to see what speaks to you. As time goes on, your career path will change multiple times. You change as a person as you gain more experience and exposure to different opportunities and industries, opening your

"The way to get started is to quit talking and begin doing." -Walt Disney

eyes to new possibilities.

If you want a more stable approach towards the end of college, applying for jobs months before graduation is a must. Applying for jobs takes a lot of effort and time. I went to school in St. Louis and applied for jobs in Dallas six months before graduation. This process was very stressful, as many employers expressed significant hesitations about me. I had not graduated yet; I was from out of state and young. It was an uphill battle explaining my worth to companies with better candidates in mind. No matter where you apply, there are a few things you can do in college to build connections and improve your chances of finding an incredible opportunity.

LinkedIn

My absolute best friend is LinkedIn for professionals. This app changed the game of job hunting and recruiting. LinkedIn gives companies access to every employee out there, making their pool of candidates incredible. The exposure also allows you to find open positions at your dream companies or companies you have never heard of.

I used LinkedIn religiously during my college days. I maxed out the potential on my account without paying for the upgraded version. I updated my profile with every position I held, with deep descriptions of what my duties were. Using good fluff

"People who are crazy enough to think they can change the world, are the ones who do." -Rob Siltanen

words to spruce up the work led to many connections and conversations. As always, never lie, but give yourself the credit you deserve. Share all the jobs you had, and write about your role using keywords that enhance the reach of your profile.

In school, you were tasked with multiple real-world projects that are incredible resumé boosters. Add these projects to your profile each time you complete one, as they are valuable experiences employers seek. You can also add skills to your profile to help highlight your strengths.

Now my favorite part: connection requests. I have found that professionals are more likely to connect with college students than someone in a similar position. It is because they understand a college student is trying to educate themselves on the industry and work they are looking for while attempting to build a web of connections. Sending simple connection requests changed my life for the better.

In my last semester of college, I wanted to build my profile as much as possible because of the number of jobs I applied to. I wanted employers to see that I was well-connected in the city of Dallas. I created a base of connections by following a few steps. First, in the search engine, I typed "Marketing," as it would bring up any person that had marketing in their job title or description.

"Man cannot discover new oceans unless he has the courage to lose sight of the shore." -Andre Gide

Next, I filtered by location and chose "Dallas-Fort Worth." When you filter by location, it shows all profiles with "Marketing" in the job title that are located in the Dallas-Fort Worth area. Then, I filtered further by position and chose everything from a director and up. Connecting with senior managers, directors, and vice presidents is the best way to make your name familiar to the people who would be doing the hiring for the job. These people make the decisions and have the most knowledge of the industry.

As you can see, the results are high. You are likely to connect with many individuals that are high up in the company if you take the proper approach. I would send a custom message to each person I felt could either give me advice or know of open jobs.

"Hello! My name is Amanda Maggiore. I am studying marketing and looking to get into the industry after graduation. I want the opportunity to learn your perspective on marketing. I appreciate your time." This simple message opened doors that never existed before. About 40 percent of those messages were replied to, and I had multiple phone calls and video chats with people in Dallas. They would share their story of how they got into the marketing world and what they liked about it. They would then ask about what I have done, why I am interested in a marketing career, what kind of marketing I want to do, and so forth.

"Start by doing what is necessary, then what is possible, and suddenly you are doing the impossible." -Francis of Assisi

I would make it a point to ask for advice on improving any skills marketers should have. Many individuals talked about interviewing, resumé building, and networking, and some offered to review my resumé for improvements and coach me on how to enhance my LinkedIn profile. These strangers were helping me succeed even though they only had one thirty-minute conversation with me. There are so many great people worldwide that are willing to help; you just have to ask!

Most people did not have jobs available at their company (this was the famous year of 2020) but said they would keep me in mind if one opened. There was one connection request that I sent and forgot about until this blonde lady with a big smile, Kristine, replied. She mentioned she was looking for someone to do some freelance blog writing. Jackpot!

Kristine and I discussed what I was looking for and what she needed help with. She offered me the contract role, and I happily accepted, knowing: 1. It is a great experience to add to the resumé, and 2. It could lead to a full-time job at that company or somewhere else. After a few months of writing blogs for her, I was praying something would come out of it. I was still applying to as many jobs as possible daily, but every opportunity ran dry. Every employer I was applying to was ghosting me, rejecting me, or simply not working out. I was losing hope as my plan to move to Dallas quickly approached. I had spent six months applying for jobs, with over 300 applications submitted. On my very last day

"I want to look back on my career and be proud of the work, and be proud that I tried everything." -Jon Stewart

of school ever, I was packing up my room when I got a call that changed my future forever. Kristine had an open position on the marketing team and wanted me to join.

I had never burst into tears so hard and so fast in my life. The stress, anxiety, anger, and frustration left my body in milliseconds, providing a sense of relief and pure joy. I could not believe I had accomplished my most challenging goal to date. I accepted a full-time position in Dallas and began my life ahead.

I often think back to that time, as Kristine and I are now great friends. If I had never sent that LinkedIn connection request, I am not sure if I would even be in Dallas today, let alone have the jobs I have had. One small move, good or bad, can impact your entire future.

"Chase the vision, not the money; the money will end up following you."
-Tony Heisch

CAREER CHECKLIST

Entering into your career can feel overwhelming. Write down some items you can check off, like updating your resumé, enhancing your cover letter, networking events, etc.

- [ ] ....
- [ ] ....
- [ ] ....
- [ ] ....
- [ ] ....
- [ ] ....
- [ ] ....
- [ ] ....
- [ ] ....
- [ ] ....
- [ ] ....
- [ ] ....
- [ ] ....

I hate to break it to you, but the skills you need in your career field are most likely not taught in the classroom. Yes, for some degrees, you must have classroom training, like a nursing degree. However, soft skills develop through life experiences and being part of the workforce. Employers are dying to get their hands on individuals that have proficient soft skills like time management, conflict resolution, work ethic, creativity, and many others. These skills are needed everywhere in the workforce because they are slowly becoming harder to find. The best way to gain more soft skills to make you a well-rounded individual is to work and put yourself through uncomfortable experiences and new jobs. Apply for jobs that might seem far-fetched or that you have little experience with but want to learn more about. The more you expose yourself to industries or career paths that pique your interest, the better you will understand where you belong and what truly makes you happy.

You cannot be in two places simultaneously, so how are you supposed to do multiple jobs? Remote work is the answer. During my last two years of college, I had several side gigs. They included social media management, website building, blog writing, and data entry, to name a few. These kept me busy and gave me the valuable experience I needed for my field. These roles gave me a foundation to build on as I entered the workforce.

Finding roles like these is easy when you use recruiting websites like Indeed, Upwork, LinkedIn, and Glassdoor. Many companies

"All you need in this life is ignorance and confidence, and then success is sure." -Mark Twain

look for interns or freelance workers to do contract work in various departments. You can take advantage of many opportunities out there that will put you ahead of your peers. Along with the experience and extra cash, there are some perks to having side roles while finishing college. You can keep these side hustles even with your full-time job for extra income as long as you can handle the workload. Also, some contract roles have the potential to become full-time roles, so doing work now could set you up for a great opportunity later on. I kept my side gigs for years after college because they were essential to perfecting my skills outside the standard nine-to-five working hours.

Working all these roles taught me one skill I never thought I would struggle with: work-life balance. You read about it in every significant publication but never think you could drown yourself in work until you do. Luckily, I caught myself dwindling in front of my laptop about four months into my professional career. I worked 12-16 hour days Monday-Friday and an additional five-plus hours on the weekend. I felt like I had something to prove to others, that I could handle a typical day job but many side hustles at once, too. I wanted everyone to see how successfully I was running my clients and making a corporate brand look good.

My schedule was exhausting. I buried myself in work so badly that I only gave myself time to eat, sleep, and work out for an hour. My weekends were usually spent doing side work,

"Progress is impossible without change, and those who cannot change their minds cannot change anything." -George Bernard Shaw

and when I did have time to chill, I felt guilty for not getting more things done. I would go to a few Texas country concerts on a Friday or Saturday night, thinking I should be at home working.

I realized that this is not the mentality to have, ever. It took me months to figure out a balance, but I slowly let myself slip out of this mindset because I was getting burnt-out fast. I hated what I was doing, which decreased my quality of work and life. When you take on a full-time position and more, prioritize yourself: your mind, health, and fun. Work will always be there, but your life won't.

You only get one life. You will miss out on all the memories there are to make if you crowd your life with work. Respect yourself enough to take a step back and look at what is consuming your precious moments daily. If you do not like what you see, make a change, as scary as it may seem. If that job keeps you from living out your best days, it is not worth it. No job should compromise your mental and physical well-being, no matter how good the job truly is. If you find yourself feeling underappreciated, overworked, or any other way of being stressed, it is time to update your situation—a change in your job, company, or even environment.

Listen to yourself and your needs as you progress through your career. Your career is a jumpstart to your life. You worked

"People often say that motivation doesn't last. Well, neither does bathing; that's why we recommend it daily." -Zig Ziglar

hard outside of school to get the job you wanted. The hard work that goes into creating a new life is substantial. You committed long days and nights to get to where you are, and you should reward yourself for that.

I am talking about time off. Many companies are known for making employees feel bad for taking time off. Whether someone is sick or it is time for a vacation, they try to make people feel guilty for taking vacation days. If you have found this to be true in your company, this may not be the best company for your well-being. Some companies encourage you to take time off because you need to reset. Taking time off work is a big boost for your mental health. Our brains cannot consistently maintain high-functioning power for long hours, five to seven days a week, and be productive. Your brain needs time to recuperate and refocus to succeed in any role.

Value your time after work and on the weekends. Spend your time doing what you want, and don't feel obligated to finish work if it is not an emergency. There are situations where you will have to work late nights or early mornings to get tasks completed, but don't make this a habit. Keep yourself in check on your hours and how often you're checking in to work, whether by email, phone calls, or simply meetings.

When you set boundaries for yourself, you'll see more productivity during the workday and less fatigue in your

"Your time is limited, so don't waste it living someone else's life." -Steve Jobs

day-to-day job. You will also last longer in your role if you give yourself the breaks you deserve. Use up your vacation days and do something that makes you happy. You don't have to go on a trip, but if it means taking a day and going on a local hike or even hanging out at the lake, do it. You have the days off for a reason, so take advantage of them. Your mind and body will thank you for the rest.

Careers will change. We are not like our grandparents, who stayed at a company for forty to fifty years and did the same duties within the same department until the day they retired. The world has changed for the better if you ask me. It is normal to be switching jobs, companies, and even career paths every three to five years. If you have maximized the potential of your position and there's no room for you to grow, it is time to hit the job applications again. If you are stuck doing the same duties each day that are not benefiting you for something better in the future, it's a waste of your life. If you find that what you studied for the past four years is not what you want to do, understand that it is entirely normal.

Finding what you want to do can be extremely difficult, and most of you are probably going through that as we speak. Start with something a little more familiar, and if you don't enjoy it as much as you thought, make the switch.

Be bold and confident. You might not have all the skills that this

"It's not about ideas. It's about making ideas happen." -Scott Belsky

career path is looking for yet; however, if you are the hardest-working and most-driven employee, you will learn quickly how to excel in the new role. Being happy with your job can change your entire perspective on life. Waking up every day excited about what you spend eight hours on can release serotonin in the brain and keep your mind thinking positively.

We all know many people in this world who are unhappy with their work, which usually rolls over to other aspects of life. If you are unhappy with what you do daily, it is time to switch. As scary as it may seem, it will benefit you in the long run.

An excellent way to get yourself excited for life outside work is to try one new thing every month. When I was settled a bit in my role, I would take the time to do something new and/or fun, so I had something to look forward to. I would find the best deals on Groupon or research events in my area. I wanted to try everything from axe throwing to a new restaurant to skydiving. It gave me something exciting to think about when I'd have those long days at work. Experiences do not have to be expensive outings, just your monthly treat to yourself for working hard and keeping yourself disciplined. Allow yourself to indulge in the fun once in a while because you have earned it.

"Unless you open yourself up to trying new things, you can't find what you love." -Anonymous

CHAPTER 9: FINANCIALS

We were all broke college kids at some point. We worked minimum wage (or multiple) jobs to pay the necessary bills. There was struggle, and some days we did not eat, but it built character, right? (Insert laughing with a bit of crying.) Some of you might still be at that point but want to get better at managing money. There are many ways to keep your financials in check and allow yourself to break free of the vicious cycle of living paycheck to paycheck.

The money you make after college is excellent. Once you get the first full-time job you have been working toward and praying for, the money is advantageous. Let's face it: many college grads do not make a lot of money right out of school. However, there are many ways to grow in your position and get the experience needed to move ranks a few years down the road to a company that will pay you more. How you manage your money starting now will determine your financial future. Let's talk about a few ways to stretch your dollar and how to keep yourself in check.

Reward Programs

There are enough reward programs for every breathing creature on this Earth. Therefore, determining what is most important to you and what will provide the most value to your lifestyle is essential. Credit cards are a necessary evil. They can build your credit and allow you to get lower interest rates on large purchases, but they can be dangerous. Credit card companies

"It's better to look ahead and prepare than to look back and regret."
-Jackie Joyner-Kersee

offer credit limits that are way too high, and their interest rates can quickly put you in extreme debt. However, if the credit card is used strategically, it can help and reward you. My number-one rule is to ALWAYS pay my card off in full each month. I avoid leaving any balance because the interest rates will increase the amount due by at least twenty percent, if not more. However, paying it off monthly should not be an issue if you stick to your budget.

Many credit cards provide rewards such as cash back, airline miles, or bonuses in gift cards. Do your research to see which company offers the best deal and wait for the annual "sales." There are big promotions when companies provide a signup bonus like 60,000 miles or $100 towards the first statement. Hundreds of companies are fighting for your attention and money, so find the right one that fits your lifestyle. I recommend always sticking with two credit cards. That way, if you ever lose one, you have a backup and are not hurting your credit score by opening many different cards. The more credit cards you have, the more it hurts your credit score. Avoid opening and closing them in a short period, as they will negatively affect your credit score. Credit cards can help you earn as you spend, so choose wisely.

Grocery stores have reward programs as well. For example, you can sign up for an account to earn points towards reduced fuel prices at places like Kroger or Sam's Club.

"Spending money is much more difficult than making money." -Jack Ma

Also, many stores send out weekly sales ads and coupons, so take the time to sift through the pile of ads to see what discounts you can find. This short time can save you a lot of money in the long run. The grocery stores will usually have a clearance section as well. Keep an eye out for these special deals, as they come and go. They can save you a good chunk of change. Shopping the sales and choosing the non-brand-name items over the big brand names will save you a good amount on your grocery bill each month.

The food industry provides an abundant amount of reward systems, like punch cards, email coupons, and loyalty programs. Many restaurants will offer a free appetizer or dessert if you sign up for their emails. They will also allow you to earn points for free food items or money off your next order. Fast food chains have apps you can scan each time you order to earn points toward a free menu item. If you like to eat out a lot, find places that will reward you for eating there and provide you with complimentary food once in a while. Use these coupons and discounts to decrease your spending on going-out meals, and get more for your dollar.

Retail stores provide reward programs through email and phone numbers, and many stores offer credit cards. If you are a shopper to a fault, one of these credit cards might be a good fit for you. Be careful with these, as they also have very high interest rates, and some do not provide the best value. If you frequently shop at

"It is great wealth to a soul to live frugally with a contented mind." -Lucretius

stores that send coupons to your email or track rewards through your phone number, you will be able to earn free items or money off your purchases. So spend less and get more of your favorite products and clothes.

To have food on the table and clothes on our backs, we must do some shopping. Reward yourself and save money on as many items as possible.

Loans, Taxes, and Banks OH MY!

Now the fun side of financials. This stuff stresses most people; unless you enjoy finance and accounting, I envy you. The financial side of life gets real when you begin to do your banking, pay off student loans, and file your taxes. These may seem like daunting tasks, but you are not alone when it comes to your personal finance.

Handling student debt, car debt, and whatever debt you have accrued over time can seem scary. Debt can hold you back from purchasing the items you want or having the financial freedom you crave. If you are wanting to become more financially free sooner in life, paying off all loans ASAP is the best way to do that. If you owe thousands in loans, set yourself up with a payment plan higher than the bare minimum. Commit to paying a more considerable amount in the beginning to pay it off quicker and make yourself financially accessible later.

"Wealth is largely the result of habit." -John Jacob Astor

Paying off debt faster will allow you to save money in the long run because you are not wasting money on interest. If you pay off your loans early, it also helps improve your credit score. Making extra payments a few times a year will put you ahead of schedule on your loans. For example, when I receive birthday and Christmas money, I make it a point to use at least one check towards my car loan. I am not saying dump all the gifts you get into your loans, however. Instead, choose a small amount that someone gave you to put towards your debt. These small payments make a significant impact on your loans.

If you are in the market for a house (look at you go!) or a new car, shopping for a loan provider is necessary to find the best interest rates. If you are looking at buying a home, shop around different banks that not only honor the first-time home buyer discount, but provide the lowest interest rates, the least amount of fees, and excellent service. Many credit unions offer great rates for loans and have fewer fees than traditional banks. You must research your area and see what provider will give you the best rate based on your credit history.

Car shopping is a tedious process as well. If you have time to shop around, wait for dealerships to have sales that usually fall on holidays. They will offer no money down, zero percent interest for the first year, or similar discounts. See what their loan providers can do for you and use them if they beat the rates of the banks you would typically go with. If not, shop the banks to see

"It takes as much energy to wish as it does to plan." -Eleanor Roosevelt

who will best fit your purchase. Again, research is key to finding the right loan for your large purchases.

Taxes can be a toughie. No matter how many TurboTax commercials I see and walk-throughs I watch on YouTube, I can never understand them. However, if you want to do your taxes, there are a few ways to go about it. Many online platforms such as TurboTax, H&R Block, and TaxAct allow you to walk through each step of filing. If you have one source of income with no dependents, this might be the move for you. Many programs teach you the process and allow you to use the services at a discounted rate or even free.

Hiring a personal tax service might be the path to go if you are an overachiever and have multiple sources of income. There are many advantages to hiring someone to do your taxes for you. First of all, you don't have to do them! You will submit all the necessary paperwork, and they will handle it for you. Also, if there is a mistake in your taxes, it does not come back on you. The fault falls on your tax filer. Having someone else do your taxes saves you from running into any trouble. Having your taxes done saves you both time and stress because they can become complicated as you increase streams of income and dependents.

Having your taxes done for you does cost a bit of money. On average, I paid $200-$400, depending on how much I had to file for the year. Many large firms will do your taxes, or if you know

"A budget is telling your money where to go instead of wondering where it went." -Dave Ramsey

someone who is certified to do so, that is even better. Ask the people you know in your area who they work with and research which option will be best for you. If you can splurge for this service, I highly recommend it. It saves a lot of headaches and worries.

We all have been using banks for years at this point. Opening my savings account as a kid was one of the most exciting feelings. Many banks offer discounts to college students and the younger generations. If you are currently banking with someone that you are not a fan of, I suggest doing some shopping. Banks do many promotions, giving you interest money or removing fees when you transfer to them. Credit unions are one of the best options to make your money go further. They have the lowest interest rates and will reward you for banking with them by giving you a few cents each year in your savings account. Find a bank with reasonable rates, high-quality customer service, and with apps that are easy to use and navigate. Do your research before switching or opening a new account to ensure you are picking the best bank for your lifestyle.

Investing

Retirement sounds like five lifetimes away from your young twenties. The last thing on your mind is saving for retirement, because you can do that "later." I am here to tell you I wish I had started earlier. You can begin investing the day you have an

"Do not save what is left after spending; instead spend what is left after saving." -Warren Buffett

income. Investing in stocks, bonds, 401k's, and Roth IRAs can set you up for life. If you become fascinated with investing, it could be your full-time job. However, if you do not become an investing whiz, you can start with the basics. Most medium to large companies offers 401k plans. Taking a little out of each paycheck is a great way to start your retirement investing. It is becoming less common, but some companies will match your 401k contribution up to a certain amount. If you invest eight percent of your paycheck, but your company matches up to six percent, you will get that additional six percent added to your investment. Watching the money disappear each month stings at first, but as you grow in your career, you realize that the money you invest now sets you up for a healthy retirement later. Your seventy-five-year-old self will thank you as you sit in your lovely retirement community, living your best bingo life.

Another great option you can begin with is a Roth IRA. A Roth can start at any point in life. Money goes into an investment account, where you can pick how risky you want to be with your money. Hundreds of companies will do this for you and point you to the right stocks to invest in based on your goals. This money will grow into the thousands as you age, and you can dip into this money early to purchase a home or other large purchases if needed. The amount will be substantial if you decide to leave it until you are retired. Roth IRAs are an easy option and a reliable one for most people.

"Do something today that your future self will thank you for." -Anonymous

The stock market and cryptocurrency can be difficult to understand. The strategy behind this is incredible, but it makes intelligent individuals a lot of money. I am here to tell you to invest, not tell you HOW to invest, because I am simply not well-informed on this subject.

There are many award-winning books to help you navigate the world of investing. Influencers and billionaires have many podcasts, YouTube channels, and other interactive content that teach you about trading. This money mechanism can have high highs and low lows. The best way to start is by researching and learning how this works. Many useful apps help you conveniently put money into the market as you wish, such as Robinhood and Coinbase. Education on this subject is critical to work the system in your favor. Through my experience and fundamental knowledge, I have made money on investments like these. I do not take it as seriously as others, but I know that anyone can make money when they invest. You could do day trading where you are on top of the markets every second or just let your money sit and slowly grow in the accounts for long-term profits.

However, if you choose to invest your money, set a monthly budget for a certain amount to be deposited into investing accounts. Then, it can spread among the different avenues available; you are not risking it all in one investment strategy. You will see the growth with time and be able to take care of your older self. Investing now is essential, as it matures over the

"How many millionaires do you know who have become wealthy by investing in savings accounts? I rest my case." -Robert G. Allen

years and can set your older self up for a comfortable life. At this age, you have the opportunity for the money to sit for decades building as the economy builds too. The more money you can invest now, the more you will have later in life.

"When you invest, you are buying a day that you don't have to work."
-Aya Laraya

What Will You Do?

It is never too early to dream of the days you don't have to work consistently. Draw a picture of the different things you want to be doing when you are no longer working. Then, write a short explanation of each.

Shop the Sales

Let's talk about smart shopping. Splurging on items you are brand loyal to or have wanted for a long time is okay to do occasionally. However, I am here to tell you that your money will go further if you can shop the sale and clearance racks everywhere. Many stores have extensive sales and clearance items for whatever you are shopping for. The grocery stores have many clearance sections with food that is a day old or about to expire. If you know you will eat it, buy it. It saves more money throughout the year than you might think.

Clothing can be pricey if you want good quality. However, we are at the age where business-casual clothes are needed daily. I recommend starting with ten different work outfits that you can easily rotate. As time goes on, you can accumulate more. Shop sales, clearance, and closeout sales for the best deals and to slowly build your wardrobe without breaking the bank. Use credit cards and reward programs to save money and get exclusive coupons. If you know you would like to have more clothes, ask for gift cards or the clothes themselves for holiday and birthday gifts. It is the best feeling when you don't have to buy your clothes; someone else does it for you!

Home decorations, furniture, cookware, and appliances can all add up if you have time to gather the items. Try secondhand stores like Goodwill to find gently used quality items.

"Recreational shopping is the shortest distance between two points: you and broke." -Victoria Moran

People are taking to online stores like Facebook Marketplace and eBay to find larger items, as many people will list high-quality, name-brand household items for a significantly discounted price. When you move into your first place outside of school, you don't need the most expensive things in the marketplace. Take the cheaper items now so you can save for the more expensive items for your future house.

Sticking to sale-priced items for whatever you buy allows you to put money towards things or experiences you want most. So find the sales, stick to your budget, and watch your accounts grow.

Renting vs. Buying

Most of us college graduates do not have the funds right away to purchase a home. Many of you will probably live with your parents for a few years, which is an excellent choice to save money. However, when you are financially and emotionally ready to leave the nest, what are your next steps to find a roof over your head?

The first step to any significant decision is looking at your financials. Can you afford to purchase a townhome, condo, or apartment? You might have the money for the down payment, but can you keep up with the bills, mortgage, and furnishing expenses it takes to live there? Considering all variables, if you feel you will be stretching your budget too thin, it is probably not

"Financial freedom is available to those who learn about it and work for it."
-Robert Kiyosaki

the best option for you. Buying is a much better financial option than renting, as you build equity in a home and can hopefully sell it for more than you bought it, but it is not feasible for everyone.

When the time comes, and you are ready for your first home, there are many programs that you should take advantage of. Many banks will give lower interest rates to first-time buyers and allow them to put down three to five percent instead of the standard twenty percent. The lower down payment opens many opportunities for you. However, be picky with your first property investment, as you only get this discount once.

Renting an apartment might be more realistic for a recent grad. Apartment shopping is fun for the first few weeks; then it becomes exhausting, making you wish someone could do it for you. Well, they can.

In this convenient age we live in, there are apartment hunters who will find the perfect apartment for you at no cost. That is correct. FREE. These apartment hunters are paid through the property management companies themselves. You must put their name down when you sign a lease for them to be paid. That said, you can contact these hunters and give them everything on your wish list, from the neighborhood to having laundry in the unit. They take your budget, find the best fit for you, and provide you with a list of places to tour and contact. If you wish to do your research, there are great sites with many apartment listings, like Zillow and

"Stay committed to your decisions, but stay flexible in your approach."
-Tony Robbins

Apartments.com. You can filter all the amenities you want to be included and by budget.

The cheapest time to sign a lease is in the off-season months. For most states, that is going to be the winter months. Fewer people want to move in the bad weather, making rent prices drop and promotions rise. If you are flexible with your move-in date, consider the winter months to get the best rate on your place. Ask the apartment complexes if they are running any deals like the first month free or adding extra service for signing the lease. Consider your work location when touring apartments because you want to be close to where you are commuting each day. There are many hidden-gem apartment complexes that you might not even know about. Many apartment building managers are looking to fill the empty units as fast as possible, making the price better for you.

I cannot stress enough to READ READ READ the reviews about the complex and units. Of course, not everyone will be positive, but it is essential to see past tenants' experiences at the complex. Reading reviews can be the difference between having either a great place to live or a total hole in the wall you are stuck in. You want to find a place that provides excellent customer service and takes care of its units. So take your time to find the suitable unit and complex for you.

"Invest with the end in mind." -Joe Saul-Sehy

Roommates

If you have a horror roommate story, I want to be the first to say I am sorry you went through that. Roommates can be very hard, both mentally and physically. As bad as it can be, some people out there make for good roommates. Whether you rent or buy, a roommate is always an option if you want to save money on your living expenses. If you feel that having a companion to live with would be best for you, I suggest going this route. Choose a roommate you know you can trust and get along with. If you are looking to room with someone that you are somewhat familiar with or not familiar with at all, there must be an open dialogue about habits, schedules, preferences, pet peeves, and other personality traits to make sure it would work for each party. Talking out all the parts of living with someone can save you from arguments in the future. Co-signing a lease means you are stuck with the apartment even if the other person decides to pack up and leave at any point. By now, you know what a suitable roommate is, so consider all the factors before making the decision.

Keeping Yourself in Check

Adulting can be very expensive. The bills begin to stack up, but you should also make time for fun. While there are many free activities out there, most things cost money. For example, if you hike one day, you must pay for the gas to get there. Therefore,

"Make sure to save for the future and keep making money!" -Jam Master Jay

you will spend your money on the most important things. After all the bills are paid, and money is in investments and savings accounts, take a few hundred a month for that to be your fun money. You can use this money to go to dinners, bar-hopping, and do fun activities with friends. Going out with friends is a beautiful thing, but highly pricy. Listen to your wallet and limit how much you spend when going out. Do you want to know the best trick for not spending money when out? Be the designated driver! Who knows, maybe your friends will buy you a drink next time for driving them.

You might feel inclined to go out because you don't want to miss out on the fun activities. First of all, if your friends make you feel bad for not wanting to join them after you explain you want to stick to your budget, they are not good friends, and you should limit your time with those individuals. Good friends will understand and support your decision.

The fear of missing out (FOMO) can be real, but if you fill your time with self-improvement activities to take your mind off other things, it will make a positive difference in your life. Rather than destroying your liver, choose to exhaust your muscles by working out. Take on a side gig and make some extra cash to invest in your future. Read books that entertain you and make an impact on your life. Make a recipe you have always wanted to try. There are many other activities that you can do that make life just a little bit better.

"What you do speaks so loudly that I cannot hear what you say."
-Ralph Waldo Emerson

Pick a certain amount of money each month you can dedicate to going out for drinks and food. Utilizing a budget will keep you disciplined and honest with your spending. You will see yourself slowly being able to save more by making minor changes to your credit card swiping habits. Trust me; your bank account will thank you when you don't buy that round of shots for the table.

Sticking to a strict budget is hard when you are right out of school. You want to do everything with your freedom, but there are healthy limits that should not be exceeded. Creating a budget does not have to be harsh; it can be more practical. Remember that everything you invest in now will be worth a lot more in the future. If you take the time to save and invest enough, who knows, maybe you can retire at a younger age.

The best way to keep track of all your expenses is to create a custom spreadsheet that works for you. Spelling out your finances will show you how much you spend on each life category, like housing, utilities, car, groceries, and fun. In addition, keeping track of spending will show you what you can save, invest, and spend extra money on. Diligence is key to success. I believe you will become financially free and independent in no time with these healthy habits.

"If there is no struggle, there is no progress." -Frederick Douglass

Income	December	January	February	March	April	May
Company 1	$0.00	$6,000.00	$3,000.00	$2,654.00	$1,688.47	$0.00
Company 2						2510.97
Company 3	$723.90	$621.14	$601.62	$742.10	$613.90	$445.80
Company 4	$0.00	$127.64	$52.13	$71.01	$92.33	$123.44
Company 5	$298.20	$168.00	$112.95	$121.71	$150.21	$139.15
Company 6	$0.00	$77.68	$77.68	$57.96	$43.39	$43.39
Company 7				$400.00	$444.00	$460.00
Company 8	$2,300.00	$0.00	$0.00		$25.00	
Total	$3,322.10	$6,994.46	$3,844.38	$4,046.78	$3,057.30	$3,722.75

Home Expenses	December	January	February	March	April	May
Rent (3rd of month)				$978.00	$978.00	$978.00
Electric (6 of month)				$49.00	$38.00	$38.00
Internet (14 of month)				$66.67	$66.67	$66.67
Food	$200.00	$200.00	$200.00	$200.00	$170.04	$149.98
Phone	$0.00	$50.00	$50.00	$50.00	$50.00	$50.00
Toiletries	$10.00	$0.00	$26.00		$56.01	
Gifting	$77.00	$123.00	$30.00		$47.55	
Going out	$62.00	$229.20	$82		$156.15	$601.71
Business Expenses	$0.00	$416.60	$30.00		$87.65	$48.55
Clothes					$15.13	
Credit Card Fees			$99.00			
Total	$349.00	$1,018.80	$516.95	$1,343.67	$1,665.20	$850.24

Transportation Expenses	December	January	February	March	April	May
Payment (paid through saving	$268.00	$268.00	$268.00	$268.00	$268.00	$268.00
Insurance (paid through check	$150.20	$144.27	$144.27	$259.27	$144.27	$144.27
Gas	$28.61	$93.31	$80.00	$100.00	$110.40	$122.80
Maintenance	$25.00	$18.00	$0.00	$10.00	$15.00	$0.00
License/Registration	$204.00	$0.00	$0.00	$0.00	$0.00	$0.00
Total	$675.81	$523.58	$492.27	$637.27	$537.67	$535.07

Health	December	January	February	March	April	May
Gym	$0.00	$100.00	$0.00	$0.00	$0.00	$0.00
Insurance	$0.00	$0.00	$0.00	$0.00	$0.00	$0.00
Vision	$0.00	$0.00	$0.00	$0.00	$0.00	$0.00
Dental	$0.00	$0.00	$0.00	$0.00	$0.00	$0.00
Perscriptions/Medicine	$13.00	$0.00	$0.00	$4.02	$0.00	$36.08
Co-payments	$20.00	$0.00	$0.00	$0.00	$0.00	$89.00
Chiro	$0.00	$530.00	$0.00	$0.00	$0.00	
Total	$33.00	$630.00	$0.00	$4.02	$0.00	$125.08

Savings	December	January	February	March	April	May
Roth IRA	$300.00	$50.00	$100.00	$100.00	$100.00	$100.00
Savings	$1,000.00					
Total	$1,300.00	$50.00	$100.00	$100.00	$100.00	$100.00

This is an example of a budget spreadsheet. There are a number of companies because, on top of my full-time job, I was receiving income from side hustles that I took on. Use a technique like this spreadsheet to keep your financials in check and look for ways to improve your personal finances whenever you can. You would be amazed how much money you will be able to save and invest when you keep track of your spending habits.

"Never spend your money before you have it." -Thomas Jefferson

CHAPTER 10: GOALS AND DREAMS

You have heard about goals for nearly your whole life. Everyone's definition of goals is different. I think goals are life's stepping stones to improving your future self. Creating goals might sound corny and cheesy, and you probably rolled your eyes when you read the title of this chapter. However, you would be amazed at what you can accomplish when you write down something to achieve. When you can visit a thought with your eyes every day, your brain is trained to work towards it.

Goals are meant to be achievable but they're not always realistic. For example, you might have a wild goal to save up $100,000 for your first house. Actions matter. Write down steps to achieve the $100,000 goal. Channel your energy and time towards the action items and watch the pieces fall into place.

Surrounding your life with reminders of your goals will lead to one accomplishment after another. These accomplishments can be both big and small, and they will vary depending on your life stage. Let's say you are going through a rough patch and are working on picking yourself up. Your goal might be to get out of bed and brush your teeth today. If you accomplish that goal, that is amazing. The step-by-step process to get to the final result will plant the seed for the future. You are training your brain to do small tasks for one common goal. If you make each day a goal, and the tasks at hand a goal, you will be unstoppable. You will watch yourself flourish in growth. Your twenties are the time to focus on yourself and do what you want and what is best for you.

"Setting goals is the first step in turning the invisible into the visible."
-Tony Robbins

Grinding things out now will pay off immensely later on. Setting yourself up at this young age will set the tone for the future. You will continue to meet goals and become more significant as time goes on. Making it a habit now to write down goals and follow through with them will be carried with you.

Think about the times in your life you worked for something. As a kid, you worked hard helping your parents around the house, so you received your allowance money. You wanted to keep working to save up for that awesome new video game. Subconsciously you had the end goal in mind—the video game. You took the steps to get there: doing chores, and earning an allowance. You have been planning goals for years without even knowing it.

Right now, separating your goals will allow you to get each section of your life under control. I am talking about career goals, life goals, self-improvement goals, social goals, health goals, financial goals, relationship goals, and any other type of goals that fit your life. Writing out goals for each part of your daily life will help narrow the focus on what you need to improve on. You can see how each aspect of life goals can make up a more incredible picture for a better you.

"In between goals is a thing called life, that has to be lived and enjoyed."
-Sid Caeser

Smart Goals

Planning out short-term and long-term goals will help you accomplish everything you set your mind to. Consistently remind yourself of what you are working towards. When setting goals, try to follow the SMART structure. Use the questions below to create your goals.

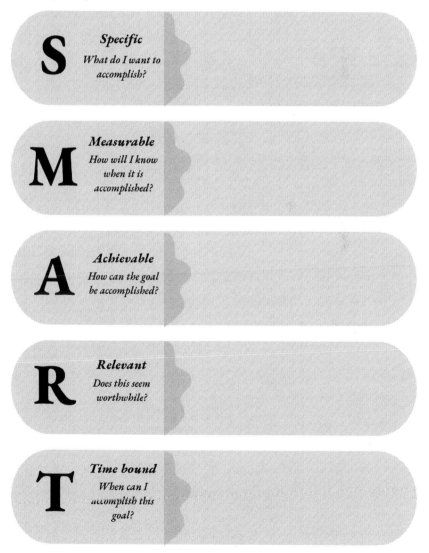

S — *Specific* — What do I want to accomplish?

M — *Measurable* — How will I know when it is accomplished?

A — *Achievable* — How can the goal be accomplished?

R — *Relevant* — Does this seem worthwhile?

T — *Time bound* — When can I accomplish this goal?

Dreams

You have had many dreams in your life thus far. You dreamt about growing up to become like your hero, your freeing teenage years, going to school, and living independently. With a few quick flutters of the eyes, your dreams have come and gone. Think about everything you have dreamt of doing and accomplishing, and look where you stand now. You should be PROUD of yourself. Even if dreams did not come true, you got to where you are. That is incredible.

It is now time to think about your bigger dreams and life-changing decisions. How do you want to live out your life? Do you want to travel the world? Make it happen. How? Set goals for yourself. Find a job that allows you to work remotely or, better yet, find a job that will enable you to travel around the world. Has your dream always been to live in an unfamiliar city? Pack your stuff and go. There has never been a better time than now to live your dreams. Dreams have a time stamp. You will not always be able to pick up and do what you want, as life will come with more limitations as you age. Prioritizing making your dreams a reality will give you the life fulfillment you never knew you needed.

There are two people in this world we need to make proud. Your eight-year-old self and your eighty-year-old self. Would mini you look up and be amazed at what you are doing, and would your

"Always nurture your inner childhood dreams, life will become beautiful."
-Invajy

future self have unforgettable memories they share with their family? If the answer is yes, then you are doing the right thing. If it is a no, put the steps in place to make it happen.

An exciting life does not have to be an expensive life. You know you have made it when you are happy with what you are doing, day in and day out, as well as pleased with who you have become, what you have accomplished, and your positive impact on others. This is how you will identify yourself when you look back years later.

Self-motivation is needed when you want to accomplish your entire list of dreams. Wishing upon shooting stars and reading tarot cards won't get you there. Discipline and hard work provide an excellent foundation to build your next move. The only person that can truly make it happen is you. You are in control of your decisions. You have the power to push yourself to make your dreams come true. Sometimes, a little outside push can help get you there. Confidence and success are contagious among successful humans. Surround yourself with people that support your dreams and want to see you live them out. These people usually have dreams they are working towards. If you are placing yourself around productive people, you will see a noticeable difference in your success rate and have a constant support system cheering you on. If you create the right mindset for yourself, it will channel your focus completely.

"A dream is a wish your heart makes." -Walt Disney

Since I was a little girl, I have always wanted to live in a big city alone. I would tell my parents, "I am not coming home after college." Gee, that was kind of harsh, wasn't it? Sorry, Mom and Dad. How does a young elementary school girl know what she will do in her twenties? I guess I was speaking my future into existence, because I made it happen somehow. I never wanted to go back to my hometown after school. It had run its course, and I was ready for something new. I worked extremely hard during my last year of college to ensure I ended up somewhere different.

By the grace of God, and after seven months of job applications, I found a job in a new city. For a while, the dream felt far-fetched after every painful moment I encountered. When the stars finally aligned, and I earned my first big girl job, I could not believe it. Living out my dream was mind-blowing because I thought I would never get there.

When you stop and look into the mirror and see that you have truly made the life that you have always wanted, the overwhelming feeling of being proud of yourself is amazing. If you can wake up every day and be proud of where you are because of the hard work you have put in, you've made it.

One of the best ways to incorporate your goals and dreams into your daily life is to write them down and make them visible to you daily. Write them down with intention. Stick them to your bathroom mirror, make them your phone lock screen, or journal

"Yesterday is but today's memory, and tomorrow is today's dream."
-Khalil Gibran

about them. There are many ways to get your ideas in front of your eyes multiple times a day.

I will leave you with one last piece of advice regarding your goals and dreams. Make a point not to share what you desire with everyone. As hard as it is, it will save you a lot of hardship and outside opinions. Talking about your future can invite others to make an opinion and judge every part of your process. Silent success is a critical piece of achieving what you want. When you share your ambitions with the wrong people, their negative words and reactions can intrude on your success. You may start to second guess yourself, doubt yourself, and think negatively about what you are looking to do. People will try to persuade you against what you want to do to see you fail or get self-satisfaction. Keeping your plans to yourself will allow you to put up barricades and only let the positive energy and momentum fuel your drive to succeed. When people see that you can accomplish what you want without validation from others, it speaks volumes about your independence.

No matter what dreams or goals you have, keep them close to your heart and allow them to guide you through life. Live your most fulfilling life, whatever that looks like for you.

"As soon as you start to pursue a dream, your life wakes up and everything has meaning." -Barbara Sher

Dream On!

Write down some of the dreams that you want to accomplish. Give yourself a time frame so you push yourself to make it happen.

Dream 1

_____
_____
_____

Dream 2

_____
_____
_____

Dream 3

_____
_____
_____

CHAPTER 11: IMMERSE INTO THE CULTURE

Whether you are back in your hometown that you swore you would never go back to or starting over in a new place after graduation, it is crucial to immerse yourself into the culture of where you're living. There is so much to discover, and human growth comes from seeing the world from a different perspective and trying new activities. Even if you think you have explored all ends of your hometown, I promise new findings await you.

Exploring new opportunities and adventures will open the mind and heart to new experiences. Frequenting the same places as you would when you were growing up will make you feel that you are trying to relive your past. Instead, make a conscious effort to go to new places and try new things. For example, try a new cafe rather than going to the old coffee shop you used to hang out at in high school. Trying new places provides a new environment and fresh faces to meet. By making a small switch like that, your mind becomes more open and comfortable going to new places and breaking routine habits. Small leaps of comfortability make a big difference when building your character and personality. Changing how your brain perceives your environment will positively influence your future. If you flood your mind with negative and repetitive old habits, there is no room to grow as an individual.

Finding the beauty of where you live is one of the first steps to enjoying the new chapter of life. People have changed slightly over the past few years, and there have been cultural shifts that

"The beauty of the world lies in the diversity of its people." -Unknown

you might not have picked up on. Exhaust all ends of the town by finding the hidden gems and corners you never took time to explore before. Meet new people, try new restaurants, find activities you have been too scared to try, and visit neighboring areas you brushed off. Adopting the culture of your surroundings will help your post-grad transition become easier. The people, the mindset, and the atmosphere around you will help shape you into the great person you want to be.

Now let's talk about making yourself really uncomfortable. Believe it or not, your brain is made for experiencing new activities. So when you shock the neurons in the brain, it not only improves memory but can also create new sparks that lead to creativity and positive emotion.

Now, I am not saying walk alone down a dark alley in the middle of the night, pretending you are excited about trying something edgy and thrilling. We need everyone to survive their twenties here. But I am saying, put some sparkle into your life.

It's all about the new things that you get yourself to do. Never felt comfortable at a workout class? Join one. It will help grow your confidence, and you will find a new way to keep your body in shape. And if you don't like it, that is okay! You practiced being vulnerable in unfamiliar situations.

"Culture is the widening of the mind and of the spirit." -Jawaharlal Nehru

Trying new things around the place you call home should be your priority. If you want constant growth, put yourself in situations where you can grow. Think about your childhood. If you never tried new things when you were young, you would not be who you are today. You subconsciously set yourself up to be the person you have become because of your actions and decisions. Immersing yourself in the culture will develop you into the person you want to become. If you do not like what is surrounding you, it's time for a change of scenery. I'm not saying you need to move across the country, but, if that is a thought, I highly encourage it. Take the time to find the places that bring out the best version of you and do the activities that make you happy.

When I traveled for work, the trips were exhausting and could get repetitive if I did not change up routines and experiences. Even though I was covering all different states, the meetings and the day-to-day work would remain the same. I kept it exciting in a few different ways.

Food is king in every city you visit. Food controls more of our lives than we realize. I would research the authentic food of the cities and states I saw, then find a local place to try the signature entrées. Every single meal I would eat would be at a local restaurant. I would do this for a few reasons. I was supporting a small business that relied on every person that walks through the door. Also, the area locals usually would

"Culture consists of connections, not of separations: to specialize is to isolate." -Carlos Fuentes

make the best food and provide fantastic service when I told them I was visiting from out of town. They were welcoming and wanted me to have an experience at their restaurant rather than eating and immediately leaving. During my stay, I would pick a restaurant from each food category to build a robust and diverse palate. The yummy food got me through the long days and made each meal exciting.

I would also book an excursion of some sort to try something new or see a popular tourist site. By creating an effort to get to know where I was visiting, it gave me a good taste of the city, the people, and what life is like as a local. Take advantage of all your situations and force yourself to do something you wouldn't always do.

"Every man's ability may be strengthened or increased by culture."
-John Abbot

How will you immerse yourself in the culture?

I AM GOING TO:

```
┌─────────────────────────────────────┐
│                                     │
│                                     │
│                                     │
└─────────────────────────────────────┘
```

I'LL ACHIEVE THIS BY:

```
┌─────────────────────────────────────┐
│                                     │
│                                     │
│                                     │
└─────────────────────────────────────┘
```

I MIGHT NEED A LITTLE NUDGE WITH:

```
┌─────────────────────────────────────┐
│                                     │
│                                     │
│                                     │
└─────────────────────────────────────┘
```

I AM GOING TO DOCUMENT THIS BY:

```
┌─────────────────────────────────────┐
│                                     │
│                                     │
│                                     │
└─────────────────────────────────────┘
```

CHAPTER 12: TRAVEL

Access to the world today is incomparable to any other age. We can go anywhere at any point at our discretion. The world is vast with endless scenery to see. Not taking advantage of what this world offers would be selling yourself short.

We all fantasize about going to different countries. At many points in our lives, we have stated how much we want to see this place and that place. How "one day" we will make it there. We all fall victim to our empty hopes. We wait until it is the right time, we have the money, and when we have the right people by our side. There will never be a perfect time. You might never have all the money saved up, and the "right" travel buddy may never come along. So why wait? If we keep waiting, the time gets away from us, and before we know it, our chances are gone. What might seem out of reach can be quite doable.

If you want to experience the world, the time is now. You will never be as free as you are in your twenties with your whole life ahead of you. So use the gifts of sight and freedom to see what is beyond your small bubble.

Traveling does have a price tag; we all know that. However, there are many ways to be able to afford to travel that you might not have considered.

I understand I am starting with the most extreme option regarding travel. However, working abroad immerses you into the culture

"Traveling – it leaves you speechless, then turns you into a storyteller."
-Ibn Battuta

quickly and opens many new doors. Small and large companies are constantly hiring foreign workers, no matter what you like to do or what you have experience in. Some jobs don't require prior experience, like working on a yacht. The opportunities are endless when it comes to finding work overseas. You can apply for visas to work in other countries, making your stay much cheaper.

After college, getting a typical nine-to-five job can be unappealing and tricky. Take three to six months to work abroad in a part of the world you have always wanted to explore. Who knows, you may love it and want to work longer wherever you end up. Now is the time to embrace new places to live and work.

If you are not looking to completely uproot your life but still want to see as many places as possible, work for a company that pays you to travel. When you are applying for jobs, start with travel companies or international companies that send employees worldwide. Jobs like this are a great way to have the trips paid for and experience new cultures. You might not be able to do and see everything you would on a typical vacation, but it is an opportunity to place your feet on foreign soil. You will get the exposure you are looking for without a long-term commitment to living there.

Let's talk about vacations. When the adult world smacks you in the face with the meager two or three weeks of paid leave each

"The life you have led doesn't need to be the only life you have."
-Anna Quindlen

year, prioritizing your days off can be challenging. There are many ways to spend your golden days, but make traveling to a new destination one of them. Make it a goal to save money and book a trip to a new destination each year. Whether that is a quick weekend trip or a ten-day expedition around Europe, find the time and funds to put yourself in a new place. Exploring new countries, people and cultures will help build your character, personality, and knowledge about the world. The eye-opening experiences shape who you will become.

Saving For Trips

Suppose you aim to go to one new place each year. Save for it. You have worked hard and deserve to treat yourself to a nice vacation. Put aside money from each paycheck to plan the trip that you have been wanting. When you give yourself a goal to save a certain amount, you are more likely to accomplish it. Make a plan and stick with it so you can fully enjoy the adventures ahead.

If you want to travel on a budget, search for the deals rather than just paying whatever price appears on the one travel website for the time frame you picked. Flexibility with travel is key to unlocking some great deals. Choose to travel during the off-season to make flights and hotels cheaper. Local businesses are looking to make as much money as possible during the off months, so they are more likely to offer more perks and

"The world is a book, and those who do not travel read only one page."
-Saint Augustine

lower prices.

Book excursions with the locals rather than large companies. It will give you peace of mind knowing the money is going directly to the people who live there, and you will get an authentic experience.

Also, utilize rewards programs. If you are looking for a credit card and love to travel, an airline or hotel credit card might be the one you need. You can earn your miles or free stays, saving you from having to purchase flights or a night or two at a hotel. Rather than going with the traditional hotel stay, look at Airbnb, VRBO, hostels, and other rental programs. They can be cheaper and provide an all-around better experience. You can make any trip you want with the budget you set for yourself. It is all about researching for the right time and checking for deals.

Growth With Travel

Traveling brings out different sides of you that you didn't even know existed. You are experiencing a world that opens your eyes to new perspectives. Putting yourself in an unfamiliar place changes your mentality and your thinking process. Your mind absorbs everything you have to see, taste, smell, feel, and hear. It can be sensory overload but in the best way possible. So travel is not only fulfilling for the soul but also nourishing to the mind. You are exposing yourself to a world far more significant than

"Travel is the only thing you buy that makes you richer." -Anonymous

yourself. You allow yourself to embrace your surroundings and truly learn what life is like elsewhere. Take advantage of the self-growth that comes with experiencing the world. After all, you only have one life to live.

"Traveling tends to magnify all human emotions." -Peter Hoeg

Travel Itinerary

Let's plan out your next adventure!

Destination:

Date:

Prioritites:

To Do:

List of Activities

CHAPTER 13: ACCOUNTABILITY

Being on your own and living out your twenties requires a lot of discipline. No one can keep you accountable for your actions besides yourself. However, holding yourself to a higher standard in this phase of life will push you to become a little better every day. You can have many people cheering you on from the outside, but if you do not have the internal motivation to make something of yourself, you'll never reach your full potential. There are many parts of life where a strong sense of willpower will pay off in the long run.

We are hot in our twenties. Think about how many people pay crazy amounts to look like they are twenty-five again. You are living in the most attractive years of your life. You are smashing. You need to take care of that body that has gotten you through each day from the start.

Some days, waking up and finding the motivation to eat healthy and work out can be difficult. Forming healthy habits now will not only improve your mental and physical well-being, but it will also carry you throughout your life. Being able to say no to friends that are going out for the fourth time this week takes courage and self-control. You know it is best for you to stay at home, cook yourself a healthy meal and save the extra cash. Keep your body young by fueling it with the best sources of energy. Develop routines that make the difference you want to see for yourself. Thinking about growing your hair out more? Research what are the best ways to do so and stick to them.

"It is not only what we do, but also what we do not do, for which we are accountable." -Moliere

Self-improvement in any form is a win, and you are practicing good habits.

Change does not happen overnight. If you wish to see a difference in yourself, you must stay loyal to your desires. Loyalty to yourself means keeping your promises, holding yourself liable for your goals, and positively impacting your life. Only you can do this. No one else can make the changes you want. Even if you have the loudest personal trainer yelling in your face, they cannot put in the work for you. Your future and your well-being lie in the palms of your hands. Do constant, honest check-ins with yourself to ensure you are keeping yourself aligned with your standards. Holding yourself to these standards may mean missing out on social events. However, if you choose to work on yourself instead of destroying your liver at the club downtown, you are already a few steps ahead of everyone else.

Following a thorough routine is necessary to earn the life you want to live. Knowing the difference between a restricting, unrealistic routine and an everyday life routine will help you set reasonable boundaries for yourself. If you feel your current routine and habits are unsustainable and impractical, it is time to switch things up.

There will always be a few sacrifices when working on yourself, but life is about balance. Food is a large category that comes to mind and influences a lot of our decisions.

"Accountability separates the wishers in life from the action-takers that care enough about their future to account for their daily actions." -John Di Lemme

My Mom taught me that when you eat healthy and work out, you deserve to have that big slice of chocolate cake or those high-calorie drinks at the bar. If you put it this way, one cupcake at night will not make you fat. One salad for lunch will not make you skinny. When you know you have worked hard, indulge in the guilty pleasure once in a while to keep yourself sane and humbled. This goes for all aspects of life. Treat yourself to that vacation, buy a pair of expensive shoes, and eat the damn pizza!

Accountability for yourself begins with the scariest place of the human body, your mind. When you are finally out on your own, you have a lot of time to think. I noticed my thoughts were a lot more active and extreme when living on my own. Not intensely, dangerously, or evilly, but in the way that they were deeper, and I read into situations a lot more.

In my second job out of school, I traveled a lot for work. I would be on long car rides all by myself, just staring at the road ahead with my thoughts. Although my travel was necessary and mandatory for my job, I realized I used it to escape my issues, emotions, and feelings at home. While staring at the endless dotted yellow line, I took the time on the road to reflect on what had been going on in my life —both the good and the bad elements, of course. Most of the time, the bad outweighed the good, which meant it needed extra attention because something was off.

"Understanding the true meaning of accountability makes us strong and enables us to learn." -Sameh Elsayed

I never knew what it was like to be in your head so much that it drives you to think irrational thoughts. You can sit there and convince yourself of things that aren't even possible just because you focus on your thoughts and have nothing distracting you from that. I quickly realized that letting my brain wander was not always the answer to my sanity.

One of the biggest lessons I learned from being on my own is to truly not overthink and overcomplicate situations. I am a naturally anxious person, and overthinking is my middle name. But as I have grown and learned, overthinking only causes more issues for me. On the solo plane rides and countless hours in the car, my mind would fixate on something that could've gone wrong, and I started to convince myself that something did go wrong. For no reason, I was making up a bad situation in my head just because I had nothing else to focus on. I learned that double-checking myself and giving myself the reassurance needed to feel comfortable was necessary to keep my mind tamed. I've noticed a lot more overthinking post-grad. I feel that life has become serious, and every decision can and will affect my future. Does this mean I will over-complicate everything?

No. I have learned to analyze a situation and make the most logical decision based on the pros and cons. That way, there is no indecisiveness and the choice made is what I live with. Even if the decision is wrong, I will hold myself accountable for it and learn from my mistakes.

"On one side of accountability is courage, on the other is freedom."
-Jean Hamilton

Emotional maturity goes a long way when trying to improve yourself. Knowing how you should react and think before you behave will set you far apart from your peers in a good way. You have standards for others, so you should be holding yourself to high standards as well. Learn to process situations before reacting and you will quickly become a more emotionally intelligent person. You are taking charge of your thoughts and emotions and not letting them steer you the wrong way. The more power you have over your thoughts, feelings, and actions, the better person you will become.

"We are all responsible and accountable for what we do or say even if those behaviors occur in stressful times." -Byron Pulsifer

Accountability Checklist

In what ways can you hold yourself accountable? Make a checklist!

- _____
- _____
- _____
- _____
- _____
- _____
- _____
- _____
- _____
- _____
- _____
- _____
- _____
- _____
- _____
- _____
- _____
- _____
- _____
- _____

CHAPTER 14: MINDSET

Putting yourself out in the adult world is scary. A doubtful, negative mind can develop when you are worried about all the aspects of life that you now face as an adult. So many forces are working against you to attempt to block you from achieving your goals. People may be telling you that you aren't going to make it to the next level, and the self-doubt gets in the way of your positive thinking. Fears creep in as you lay still after a long day of doing something you don't love.

Constant negativity about yourself and your situation changes how your brain thinks and works. We have all met somebody negative with almost every sentence that comes out of their mouth. Nobody enjoys being around them because it is draining and puts a damper on the entire environment. Negativity spreads like wildfire because once a person is down, they look to bring others down so everyone can be on the same playing field. A negative brain can consume your life if you are unwilling to change your thinking pattern. In this chapter, we'll talk about the negativity in your life and how it should be addressed.

Excuses

We have all made excuses in our lives for just about everything. We have found reasons not to do something that we probably should have or made up a white lie to escape a situation we did not want to be in, good or bad. While figuring out your life and getting on your path, you will catch yourself making excuses for

"Excuses will always be there for you, opportunity won't." Anonymous

things you want to do.

"I am too tired. I am too busy. I don't want to waste my money."

Excuses have a drowning effect on your thinking patterns. If you are a chronic excuse-maker, you will find a way out of every situation and completely derail your path in life. If you make excuses each day to not better every aspect of your day, what kind of life are you setting up for yourself? Of course, there are valid excuses like if you have come down with an illness or something tragic has happened. But these excuses can only last so long. You must tell your brain that these excuses will not run your life.

If your mind is looking for that saving grace excuse any time you get into a situation that you are unfamiliar with, recognize it and go against what your inner thoughts are telling you to do. Make the leap of faith to do something that makes you physically and mentally uncomfortable.

Excuses cause you to sell yourself short of experiences in life. For example, let's say you don't believe you should waste your time applying for a job because they are looking for five years of experience, and you only have two.

Apply for it regardless and show them why you deserve to have that role. What sets you apart from someone who has that five

"Your excuses are just the lies your fears have sold you." Robin Sharma

years of experience? Sell yourself and prove that you are the best candidate for that role. If you continue to doubt yourself and find a way not to reach for the moon with every decision you make, you will live an unfulfilling life.

Maybe you're tired of living at your parents' home and ready for your own place. But you feel like you don't have enough money to live on your own. Throw this excuse aside by setting up a budget and seeing how much you genuinely need to afford to live. Remember that humans only need the bare necessities; shelter, food, and water. If money is a reason you are not moving out, fix it. Think about how much access you have to new jobs and work. There are thousands of remote jobs, and many companies hire part-time workers for all positions. Push yourself to work an extra job to be able to make your dreams a reality. It will be hard work and take much dedication, but the fulfillment you get from having your own place and creating a stable life for yourself is priceless.

You are given one life, and the most precious gift of your life is YOU. So commit to discarding excuses from your vocabulary and work through situations by pursuing every opportunity with an open mind.

Fears

Fears are crippling to human growth. How will you ever

"Ninety-nine percent of all failures come from people who have a habit of making excuses." -George Washington Carver

experience the unique parts of the world if you live in fear? Don't get me wrong, there are legitimate fears, like my fear of snakes. They send my anxiety through the roof, even just seeing one slither along the path I walk every day. UGH. I know that snakes will be around every time I take a walk on my favorite path each day in the spring. But just because I know snakes will be slithering by my ankles at any given moment, I do not let it hinder the walk I take each day after work. That walk is therapeutic and essential to my mental health.

I have mastered this fear by remaining calm when I see one and quickly walking by without making a fuss. The more I have this mindset each time I see one of the devil's animals, I get a little more relaxed when the situation does occur. I have noticed that my anxiety doesn't skyrocket each time, and I can handle being in nature while enjoying myself. P.S. No offense to anyone that likes snakes or has a pet snake. They are just not for me.

Now, that is just a surface-level fear. How about more significant fears like death, failure, and the unknown future? Allowing these fears to consume your daily thoughts will restrain what your life has in store for you. You will not accomplish your goals because of the limitations you are putting on yourself. Make bold moves, like trying something you have always wanted to do, or test your comfort levels with adrenaline-seeking activities. If you let fear define you, you will live your life in a tiny cage. Your ability to become an improved version of yourself is put at risk if you

"Fear defeats more people than any other one thing in the world."
-Ralph Waldo Emerson

allow fear to control your thinking process. We all want to enrich our souls, but if you let the heaviest doubts cast a shadow on your future, the chances of changing your life are slim to none.

Taking a big or small chance can be the life-altering decision that guides you for most of your days. It paralyzes you when you are overly cautious because you do not want a tragic event to happen. It disables your chances of pursuing precisely what you want to do because you are thinking of all the bad things that could happen. When you overanalyze and think of every "what if" scenario, you create fictitious events, sending your mind into panic mode. The best piece of advice I could give you, don't think. This time in your life is when you should not be thinking about your crippling fears. Instead, you should overcome them subconsciously by putting yourself into situations out of your comfort zone. Overcoming your worries will be one of the most significant accomplishments of your life if you allow yourself to get to that point. Of course, it takes work and courage, but after everything you've endured up to this point, there's no reason why you can't accomplish and overcome what is holding you back.

I was inspired by a friend telling me I should turn my fears into positive affirmations. Not only does it positively alter my thinking patterns, but it helped me conquor some of my most destructive fears. Write down what you fear most and how you will overcome these fears with positive words and actions.

"Everything you want is on the other side of fear."
-Jack Canfield

FEARS CHART

What are your fears in life? What positive affirmation can you use to overcome each fear? What actions can you take to become brave?

FEAR	THOUGHT	ACTION

Worrying

The unknown world worries us all. The future holds more than we can imagine, and we don't even know a lick of what is going to happen five, ten, or even fifteen years from now. But unfortunately, worrying about what you cannot control does not improve your situation.

I learned that worrying crushes your daily thoughts, actions, progress, and relationships. I grew up as a worrywart. I fully admit it. I'm stressed about anything and everything under the sun. I was worried I would do something wrong to make my boyfriend leave me, worried I messed up at my job, worried about what other people thought of me, and worried about not being successful enough, to name a few. Looking back on these worries, some still appear from time to time. However, there is no reason for these to dictate my life and run my thought process. My worrying got so bad that it would cause panic attacks. I would stress about the dumbest situations, sending my mind spiraling into creating unrealistic conditions. I was worried about too much that was not in my control.

If you let worry conquer you, you will never be content and at peace. The concerns will eat away at your internal light, forcing dark thoughts into your head and overanalyzing everything sending your physical and mental health down the drain. The lasting effects of worrying can be catastrophic to your growth as

"Worry pretends to be necessary but serves no useful purpose" -Eckhart Tolle

an individual.

It is okay to have concerns about how your twenties will play out. It is the stage of life where everyone is confused about what is going on and what needs to happen. Many unexpected changes will alter your initial course of life.

But consistently worrying about the outcomes of every situation will do you more harm than good. It will train your brain to go into panic and stress when thinking about how something will end up. When you feel negative and worrying thoughts enter your mind, counter them by reminding yourself that you cannot control what is out of your hands and every event in your life happens for a reason.

Learn how to take control of your thoughts and turn doubt into something positive by using gentle words. Proactively work on speaking and thinking more positively and you will see your worrying slowly begin to fade. Everything will turn out how it is supposed to, and worrying changes nothing.

When I worry, I replay my grandmother's voice saying, "Take a breath, Gracie!" because she knew I would stress about simple things. I actively remind myself that one deep breath can go a long way.

"Whatever is going to happen will happen, whether we worry or not."
-Ana Monnar

Accepting The Past

Forgiveness means giving up the hope that the past will be different.

We all have endured tough situations in life that are hard to accept. Whether that was someone who did us wrong, left us behind, or severely damaged our mental and physical health, we all know what it feels like to be hurting. Your past has created who you are today. Some moments were extremely difficult, while others were fun and carefree. The past can hold on and linger for so many days that it inhibits the ability to move forward with a new life. To carry on each day, you must forgive the past.

Many of us think that forgiving means forgetting what has happened in our life. Forgiving someone or something does not mean forgetting what pain they or it caused you, but it is accepting that what has happened can never be changed. The damage done cannot be reversed. We hold onto heavy grudges and anger in our life because we are unwilling to accept that there is no longer a chance that the past will change. We believe if we stay angry and hold this emotion against the person or situation that hurt us, somehow it will change to make us feel better.

I truly struggled with forgiveness on a few different occasions. A guy I had dated had left deep, painful wounds in my soul and

"It's not about getting over things, it's about making room for them. It's about painting the picture with contrast." -Brianna Wiest

mental state. I had never been put through hell emotionally like I was with him. At the time, he had destroyed me. I felt I had lost myself in many ways, and I let his narcissistic actions and words blind me from what was truly happening. I could not believe what he had put me through, and the pain was nearly unbearable at times. I held so much anger and hatred because it felt like no matter what I did, there was always a piece of him still with me that I could never shake. It took nearly a year to fully start to come to terms with what I had endured. And I could not do it alone. My incredible friends and family helped me realize that forgiving him would finally allow me to move on with my life. They stayed up late to listen to me cry, were there for me at my lowest points, and made me realize how much better off I was even after going through a brutal relationship.

I learned my lessons the hard way, and I decided to move forward with my life and grow in every way I could.

Growth comes to those who accept what they have endured and those who learn from the past to ensure there are no repeats in the future. Forgiving the past brings peace over your heavy heart and allows the next chapter to begin in your life. Forgiveness no longer gives someone power over our emotions. Taking your control back starts with letting go of what you have been holding on to. Once you have taken your time to heal and fully accept your fate, your happiness will start to flow, and your big heart will shine again.

"The weak can never forgive. Forgiveness is the attribute of the strong."
-Mahatma Gandhi

ACCEPTING THE PAST

Holding on to the past prevents your growth. What are some past events that have affected you in some way, and how will you overcome this situation for good?

Past Experiences	How To Move Forward
1	☐
2	☐
3	☐
4	☐
5	☐
6	☐
7	☐
8	☐

Indecisiveness

Indecisiveness is the insecurity of making your own life. If you cannot make a simple decision about where to go to dinner or where your next trip with your college besties should be, how are you capable of making decisions that will significantly impact your future? How can you build trust in yourself to make the right decisions in the most critical moments? Not being able to make your own decisions promptly will steal your enormous opportunities in life. There is so much waiting for you, but you are one indecisive thought away from ruining what could be a dream come true.

When making impactful decisions, take the time to think about all the pros and cons that go to both sides. Draw up all the facts and points to consider for each situation. Once you feel that you have thought out every part of both sides of the decision, give yourself twenty-four hours to make the decision and stick with it.

The longer you wait and go back and forth, the more likely you are to doubt yourself and to lose trust in your ability to make your own decisions. Go with what your gut says and decide to stick with the option that you choose. The longer you wait and go back and forth, the more likely you are to doubt yourself and to lose trust in your ability to make your own decisions. Go with what your gut says and decide to stick with the option that you choose.

"Action cures fear. Indecision, postponement, on the other hand, fertilize fear." -David Joseph Schwartz

The option that you choose might be the wrong option for you. But you won't know it until you're fully in the situation. But do you want to know the beauty of making the wrong decision? It is experiencing something that gives you tools, skills, and knowledge to ensure that the same decision is not made again. You now have a new life lesson under your belt that contributes to your growth as a person. Making your own decisions is a huge privilege as you grow through your twenties. Many people don't have the choice to make self-improving decisions on their own. Recognize how lucky you are to be able to pick your path in life.

A great way to practice making decisions is to use social settings as your foundation. If your group of friends is talking about where to go for happy hour and people are throwing many options onto the table but no one is picking one, make the executive decision of where to go. Being a decision leader even in the smallest ways can help you gain confidence in making choices faster. If you find yourself debating whether or not to do something, make the decision quickly, stick with it, and do not second-guess yourself.

Enemies

The people that want us to fail the most are the most motivating. Think about the people that have exited your life for whatever reason; they are hoping you fail. They want to see you fall flat on your face because they don't see what truly lights your fire.

"Be decisive. A wrong decision is generally less disastrous than indecision."
-Bernhard Langer

Use the doubters, the instigators, and the bullies as fuel to do well in life. Prove to people that you can create a purposeful future. Success is the sweetest revenge. Make something of yourself so they can never forget what you have done. Your enemies will watch closely, just waiting for the moment you slip up, so give them the perfect show. Once you succeed, envy will fill their minds as you become an inspiration.

But what about those enemies and demons you can never get rid of? The ones constantly talking to you even when you try to bury them deep. I am talking about internal enemies. The subconscious thoughts that sit there and put you down. The ones that make you overthink and second-guess yourself. That voice screams at you for everything you have done wrong and won't allow you to move on. The internal enemy is the harshest of all.

Part of growing up is conquering this enemy. Those doubts are foreigners in your mind. Finding ways to alter your thinking patterns to exclude negativity can change your daily life. When you fight your inner demons and muster up all the energy and motivation you have to accomplish growth, you will quiet those voices forever, permanently changing how you view yourself.

Perseverance

This section goes out to my mom. While I was writing this book, without her knowledge, we were discussing how perseverance is

"Your friends will believe in your potential, your enemies will make you live up to it." -Tim Fargo

learned heavily through college. Now, this might be the truth to a degree. In college, we know to push through the challenging classes even if that class provided no value to our life. That is perseverance, but it's also "playing the game." Playing the school game involves some strength, but at the same time, it consists of much compliance with what society says to do. Of course, you work hard and push through to get to the final goal, but I believe perseverance comes from many other stages of life.

Tragedy, loss, and pain in other experiences create who we are as people and teach us to work through our problems. Whether internal battles or external issues, we have learned to get through every roadblock that has come up in our life. Many more significant issues and problems arise in life than in a class.

Many of us have struggled with internal demons and have learned to fight our own battles. We push through the depressing days even when we feel no end in sight. Deciding to wake up every single day and face the challenges ahead is perseverance in itself. Realizing when you are in a deep rut and clawing your way out of it on your own to get to a happier and safer place: now, that is determination.

Putting the past behind you and opening your mind to the future is dedication. You must actively remind yourself to be better than you were the day before. Deciding to be the best version of yourself takes extreme guts.

"Keep the faith, don't lose your perseverance and always trust your gut extinct." -Paula Abdul

Everything you have fought through has given you a little more drive to keep going. Your confidence builds as circumstances and life events occur. You have shown extraordinary courage, even when you wanted to give up. Instead, you choose to work through everything put in your path and create a life for yourself with the lessons you have learned.

Perseverance develops a whole new meaning as you grow older. Life challenges get a little bit harder. People who you thought would stick around leave. Financials become a reality quickly, and developing a life you want can become difficult at times. You must fight through the pressure that others are putting on you, and the force of perfection you put on yourself.

You are strong, and because you have thrived up to this point, you will kill it in this next stage of life.

Everything Happens For A Reason

Is this phrase overused? Yes, yes, it is. Does it actually make sense, and is it true? Also, yes. I never realized how much this phrase rang true until I lived independently. A lot changed in a short amount of time making me question why. People came into my life and for some of them, I truly wondered why they were placed there. When opportunities for work came up and they didn't work out, I never understood why. But to counter that, when something amazing happened, I would ask myself why I

"Let me tell you the secret that has led to my goal. My strength lies solely in my tenacity." -Louis Pasteur

am lucky enough to have this moment.

That *why* question. We want to know the reason behind every event in our life. We long for an explanation so we can rationalize it in our minds. Sometimes, we will never understand or know why we go through the things that we do. Other times, we will slowly begin to comprehend the why. But no matter what comes and goes in our life, that is how it is meant to be.

Your life is already determined for you. Good or bad, every event coming down your path is preplanned by decisions today. You have made choices in. the past that have led you to this point. Your twenties are the time to consciously make the best decisions to shape your life. You have the world at your feet and can now take advantage of your circumstances. Realize that it is meant to happen no matter what you go through. You are meant to be right where you are.

"I knew everything happened for a reason. I just wished the reason would hurry up and make itself known." -Christina Lauren

CHAPTER 15: LIVE YOUR BEST LIFE

College will be a stage in your life that you look back on and smile about. While you learned a little about your career field, there is still so much left to learn in the big world. You will make mistakes, you will grow into a whole new person, and best yet, you will begin to live the life that was meant for you.

Go out and do what you want. You are creating your own story and no one but you can write your beautiful book of life. You have made it this far; why not make the rest of your days count for something?

I hope you feel a little more ready to enter into your next chapter. Take the lessons learned from this book, friends, family, and past experiences, and embrace every opportunity that comes your way. Love deeply, live freely, and never forget how much you mean to this world.

I believe in you. New beginnings are ahead. Run full speed into the wind and let your next chapter begin.

It's time to live your best life!

"You only live once, but if you do it right, once is enough." – Joe Lewis